Becoming King of the Nerds

How to Run IT Teams and Influence People

Rob Hogarth

This book is dedicated to my wife and my children, who help me to remember there is more to life than technology.

Preface

Τhis book is written by a self-confessed nerd who after years of loving technology learned that talking to people could be far easier and more effective.

My hope is that this book is interesting, instructive, and insightful for you as you aim to grow in your career. There little to no thought given to technology but rather to the non-technological side of IT. The little discussed but highly important aspects of being an IT person or working in an IT team of any sort.

I aim to provide my own thoughts and feelings on IT and business through my own experience in my own way. You may disagree or find certain things don't apply to you. The only thing IT people will agree on is that no two IT people will ever agree on anything. IT is a varied field that works within every single type of company; therefore, your direct application or experience may differ. At the very least I aim to start a conversation in your own mind about your management style, your career and your interactions with your colleagues. Agreement in all aspects is not necessarily an objective.

I would like to apologise to all my former colleagues and especially managers who probably wish I knew all of this when I worked with/for them.

Contents

A Word Concerning Nerds

We are a strange folk., those of us who work with computers. The nerds, the true nerds, we love technology. It makes sense to us. We can learn and understand it. We can visualise in our heads how electrons move through the computer. We see TCP/IP packets flow through the network. We scan files 1000s of lines long and quickly pick out the errors. As they say in the movies, we don't even see the code anymore.

As teenagers, we tinker and play. We pull things apart to figure out how they work. We change settings on computers just because we can. Our curiousness doesn't manifest in the exploration of the outdoors and the beyond. It focuses inwards, to CPUs and memory to wires and components, bits and bytes.

People get into IT for one of two reasons. First, they are nerds. They LOVE the technology. The second group of people get into IT because it pays well. Or at least they think it pays well.

I'm only going to deal with the first group.

Computers, we love them. I'm a nerd. If it has electricity in it, I understand it. I know how it works. I know why it works. Why it doesn't work. Give me an engine and I'm lost. Sure, I know the overall concepts, fuel + air + spark = boom + movement. But I don't KNOW it. And if it's broken, I can't fix it.

Give me something IT worthy. A computer, a phone, a printer, a switch, and I instinctively know what to do. You either are one of these people or you aren't. It's not a brag or a boast, it's just how our brains work.

As a kid, you start with the technology you have at home. If you're older like me that means writing software into your computer, Commodore 64, Amiga or PC equivalent.

The Internet? What's that? Nothing like that existed for kids like us.

Oh no, you programmed by copying pages of BASIC from a magazine. You and 4 other guys at school trade games on floppy disk, sharing secrets on how to get through that next section in King's

Quest[1]. You somehow obtain a hacked copy of Street Fighter[2] with special moves.

The internet[3] connected everyone. We all became experts at dialup and how to configure it. If you are a little younger, then you skipped this step and when straight to configuring home routers and the basics of networking.

Finally, as you approach the end of high school, you realise the HTML code, the BASIC, all the times you fixed computers for your neighbour or uncle or whoever, is something that could lead into some sort of career.

So, after you complete your education you step out into the corporate world.

I hate to generalise, but I'll make this one exception[4]. I'm going to suggest this about IT people in general:

They are smart.

The IT department are among the smartest people in any organisation. The good ones are. But I'd say we are overall higher than average. We have a

---

[1] I still have the Kings Quest Companion on my shelf.
[2] 3 different types of Hadokens
[3] Yes, the internet existed for some time before the mid-90s when I started using it, but 94/95 was still pretty early in Australia for our house to be "online".
[4] I'll make no apologies for doing it again later.

specific type of natural ability. IT people understand abstract concepts extremely well. That's why we can visualise those electrons well. We identify trends and patterns very quickly. I read logs files like you read the newspaper. We can look at information and form an outcome or opinion quickly.

But IT people are terrible at working with people[5].

Computers are fast idiots. They will very quickly run any program we write. The computer will add two numbers, extremely quickly and always be correct. Although, a computer doesn't know if it's the right two numbers to add. However, there is an enormous amount of consistency.

Hence A plus B always equals C, no exceptions[6].

And we love that. It appeals to our brains in a very primal way. The way we are constructed loves the consistency of technology. It is the ultimate truth that we build everything from it.

In contrast, people are fickle and unpredictable. This directly contradicts the beauty of consistency and thus breaks our brains.

Nerds don't know how to handle people. There is limited predictability and thus working on a problem a technical solution is always superior to

---

[5] IT people are also terrible at other things including, talking to girls, letting something go even though they might be right, and sports.
[6] Also 2+2=5 for *extremely* large values of 2

a solution that involves anything that would involve communicating with people. Even if working with people would give a better outcome. It's not something most nerds would even think about.

Thus, the eternal problem.

A child with technological interests, works through school years to develop said interest. While they enter the workforce with good computer skills and focus on developing them further. They can have limited interpersonal skills and do not work on those. In fact, they see little to no value in them.

Thus, this child is now an employee and presents challenges from a management perspective. Worse still, this employee can be thrust into management with no helping hand.

This all might seem like a negative view of IT people. However, I think it's important to understand where a lot of IT employees come from, what we like and dislike and therefore how to manage us or evolve.

Not all IT people are exactly alike. But I see a lot of people getting into this field the same way. We love technology because it suits our brains.

Understanding this is a key to understanding IT people.

This isn't to say our personalities are all the same. Is every IT guy a genius? No, just a chosen few. There are some people in IT that would cause you to wonder how they tie their shoes in the morning[7] Some of us are health nuts, run marathons and spend hours at the gym. Some of us spend too much time at the Pokémon gym instead.

However, there are, I feel, more similarities than differences. A lot of us are introverted and quiet. A lot of us are nicely described as socially awkward. We have ADHD or are "on the scale" as they say, of autism. We spent nights playing games online. We have our own culture and language.

While some people find this weird and strange, I love it. I love being in IT departments with people, making the jokes nobody else gets, working at the speed of light on problems where others can't keep up. We are special. We are valuable.

Nerds built iPhones and iPads. Nerds created the internet. Nerds have brought about every significant change in the world especially in the past 40 years[8].

We need to great IT leaders to help show how amazing we are. Those IT leaders need to come from within our midst. Not an outsider.

---

[7] Wait…. these are loafers.
[8] The ability to view millions of cute cats instantly on a handheld device is something future cultures will marvel at

But we only become great when we understand our strengths and weaknesses and how we can harness them.

The Core Problem

I 'm going to propose a fundamental problem that all IT people will relate to, but most won't comprehend the implication of.

People don't understand what "IT" does

There's a second follow on fundamental problem:

Most people don't care what "IT" does as long as it just "works"

Those two concepts are the core of every challenge in IT today.

No matter how great you are, most people you work with and know don't understand what you do and they don't really care.

That's a tough reality to deal with. But no job is easy, and this is our burden.

Consider the following all too familiar scenario:

New employee starts on a fresh Monday morning.

There is a process for new user creation.

Nobody has followed it.

You were not made aware of this fact.

This is not unusual.

You are approached mid-sip of coffee with a manager and new employee, who both interrogatingly ask:

> *"Why hasn't my new employee got a login!"*

Before you can swallow your mouthful of coffee to reply, the new employee remarks:

> *"This is just like IT at my last company they could never get anything right either!"*

They both storm off. Hopefully, I haven't given anyone PTSD flashbacks.

> "This is every day in my world". *I can hear you saying.*

Unfortunately, it's far too common. Our response as IT staff is to become defensive:

> *"There's a procedure to get new accounts!"*

Of course, there is. It's probably a great one, well thought out, well implemented, and properly communicated to the office.

At lunch time we get derisive:

"That new employee doesn't even do anything important, and we dropped everything to get her setup!"

Most likely this is where we end up. Everyone is unhappy.

The company doesn't value you. It doesn't understand why you developed a process and will never follow it. You never feel respected or feel like you are contributing at your capacity. Ultimately the stalemate continues until you leave.

> **People don't understand what IT does, and most people don't care as long as IT just "works"**

This is the biggest problem you will face, and the biggest challenge you need to overcome.

Part of this issue stems from a complete lack of understanding of just what corporate IT teams do.

We inherently have a picture of what people in companies do based on our own experiences. We have a picture of salespeople as outgoing Type As in suits, sleazy used car salespeople, or the tired door-to-door salesman travelling around selling his wares.

Whether you envisage poor old Gil Gunderson from the Simpsons[1] or Alec Baldwin from Glen

---

[1] Old Gil needs you to tell all his friends to buy this book.

Garry Glen Ross, we all have some idea of what a salesperson does. Even if our idea isn't entirely correct.

Same thing for the finance team, we pay our bills and do taxes, so we may feel corporate finance is inherently like our own experience, but company bills are larger, and they probably pay LESS tax with some smart accounting tricks unbeknown to us.

This reasoning is obviously incomplete but good enough to give us some idea of the skills, tools and abilities required for each role.

> *"Oh, I'm not outgoing enough to be in sales" "I just don't have the numbers for finance!"*

Some of these fields are easy to view and understand. Old Gil is a terrible salesperson because he doesn't sell things. Alec Baldwin was selling lots of houses and drove a great car. You either sell lots of *things* and are great or sell nothing and are terrible.

Likewise, if you're in accounts payable and never pay anyone, you are probably not doing things right.

But this doesn't translate to every field. We all have been in positions where we are quite critical of our CEO/General Manager. They never do any REAL work. They are never in the office. They are overpaid and under-qualified. For some CEOs that may be an entirely valid criticism. But a lot of people don't have an appreciation for what a CEO actually does every day. WE get a little older and start to have our own teams, or our own family that we are responsible for, and start to get an appreciation for it.

Running a company can be a real tough job. You have the ultimate responsibility for millions of dollars or hundreds of millions or even more. 1000s of people can rely on them for their very livelihood. Those times they show up seemingly late probably hide the early morning meetings they had after the work-related dinner that they presented at. The food is great, but there's some long hours and speeches and discussions that can easily sway a whole business very quickly.

Swings and roundabouts as they say.

We start off in our teenage years seeing bosses being portrayed as entitled, layabouts, earning the big bucks and having the high life. We see the Mr Burns', the Michael Scott's and the Bill Lindbergh's of the world. They exist in a black and white world of corporate greed, employee indifference and entitlements. Hopefully, as we grow up a little and see the Dr Perry Cox's and the Captain Raymond Holt's and the Sherman T Potter's. They exist in a grey world, where things are never just right or wrong. The Jean-Luc Picard, the greatest Captain of them all[2] said it best:

> It is possible to commit no mistakes and still lose. That is not a weakness... that is life.

---

[2] You heard me.

If we apply this to IT teams, we can see parallels. The most obvious is that a naive view of IT is that it's just like fixing an iPad at home. Or if someone is super adventurous, building a PC from parts they bought at a PC store, case + motherboard + CPU + PSU = ultimate gaming PC[3].

As IT professionals, we scoff and laugh. Building PCs is nothing like what we do. Of course, this is true, we buy computers 50 at a time from Dell, or rack 1ru rack mount "*pizza box*" servers like they are indeed pizzas. We know, IT is far more than simply desktop hardware. Its more than just clicking next next next in an install wizard, or having a recording that declares "Hello IT, have you tried turning it on and off again".

But the great reality is, nobody will ever understand the scope, detail, care and forethought that goes into running a successful IT team unless we as leaders are the ones who help to identify this.

There's also definitely an art to this. I might be super excited that I've fixed a very difficult issue that's taken me days to resolve. On a high in the break room, I go to explain what I did, but get glazed eyes and a complete lack of understanding. Especially from senior managers. They might get bored quite easily at an intricate technical explanation.

---

[3] Just like Linus Tech Tips, but without the crazy budgets and sponsored parts

Maybe our colleagues can humour us a little and be happy for our success without understanding it.

However, what if the problem I solved can boil down to "I fixed a problem with increasing redundancy (…boring so far), which prevented us having downtime (…ok I get that bit) which saves us $100,000 per hour in the event of a power outage". OK, now you've got someone's attention.

However, giving people an appreciation of the scope of IT teams is one thing. The real issue here is more than just understanding why IT is important.

There's a certain level of entitlement and trust that can go with an IT team. The late-night work, the weekend changes, the out of office upgrades, that means a lot of the time we are rolling into work late in the morning with the CEO, hours after everyone else has arrived. Or we are out of the office on training, or speaking, or working with a vendor. All legitimate excuses for being out of the office.

But what do those other teams around us think? Do we even let them know why we were in late? Most likely because we were up late making sure systems were going to be working smoothly **for** them.

This can be an epic source of contention in the office. We work hard, sacrificing our late nights and weekends. But our users just see the half days, the early marks, and the seemingly random approach to being in the office. After all of this the

IT team get praised for their good work? They are hardly ever here!

If you want to be a successful IT manager and above, you need to understand these issues. But more than that if you want to be successful in IT full stop, you need to start to understand and embrace these challenges.

Break down the walls, start building bridges.

Or in other words, if you want some respect and understanding, you might need to be the person and team to start giving some of those things out.

Who wants to be a CIO?

Do you have what it takes to be a manager? Do you really? Are you being forced into a senior role when you like being hands on? Do you still love to dig around in server rooms and data centres? Do you love writing code? Could you give that up?

Importantly, do you enjoy meetings?

I'm not sure anyone truly enjoys meetings. So let's ask some different questions

Do you like working with people even those outside your team?

Can you create strategy and vision, and communicate them effectively?

Do you enjoy mentoring junior colleagues?

Most importantly

Can you be a part of the "Management Club"

What? There's a club? Yes, there is. It's a magical place, of long lunches on a Tuesday, drinks on a Friday and golfing every Thursday morning. Oh, you thought your Sales manager had meetings on Thursday morning? He did. They are on the golf course.

There is an executive club. It's not just an airline lounge type thing, although yes, that is indeed part of it. If you want to be an IT manager, Director or even CIO, you need to prove to people inside the club that you can be part of it.

This importantly is making sure you fit in with the club rules. They aren't published anywhere, and their change can be seemingly random. Importantly everyone in the club can identify if you're breaking any of the rules.

Sometimes we can join the club by accident:

**In the Simpsons, Homer
grows hair, and by
happenstance joins the club.**

**In Apple during the early
1980s, a technical guy noticed
all executives had
moustaches. He announced to
colleagues he would grow a
moustache. The day he
pronounced it as "complete"
he promoted into the club.**

One of these stories is on TV the other is real life.

Club rule 1: Look the part.

Do you come to work dressed in a t-shirt and jeans? Does the CEO? I thought not. If you want to be in the club wear what the club members wear. Contrary to what you might think, there is a dress code. It's not necessarily published.

I've written about this before[1] and people get very upset. A tie! Never! Ok, you can try and get into the club without a tie, because your workplace is hip and cool. I doubt it, but maybe it is.

I'll give you more of a guideline then:

Make more of an effort in your grooming

A t-shirt without holes, even a fitted t-shirt. A tie that isn't a novelty tie. A haircut that costs more than $10. The point is you need to make an effort. The people in the club are in charge. So mostly they dress like it. Managing millions of dollars isn't something that guys in sweatpants do.

Your image matters.

The more seriously you take your image in the workplace the more you will automatically be

---

[1] Reddit.com/r/sysadmin – Some of those guys really did not like the idea of ties.

taken seriously. If it sounds dumb, then you just have to trust me.

But remember our core problem *"Nobody knows what you do".* This is our first step in addressing that problem. Dress like you do something important. Dress like you have value.

And I know that Mark Zuckerberg dresses in jeans and a t-shirt. But he's a billionaire, plus his t-shirts are $1,000 each not $10 from Target. So even he makes an effort. Even though he tries not to make it look like he tries.

My basic rule here is step everything up a notch. If you wear a collared shirt, try a tie or a jacket or both even just a few days a week. If you already wear a suit, make sure it's a nice one, and it's tailored. Buy a nicer pair of shoes. Polish those shoes. Wear cologne, not just deodorant. Seriously, you wear deodorant, right?

If you need help ask your wife, girlfriend, sister, or mum to help you. Find the guys from Queer Eye to give you a makeover. Watch what celebrities[2] with your body shape wear.

Or in all seriousness get a professional style consultant to help you. Many executives do. It may help you a lot if you have a workplace that is between casual and formal. A formal workplace is a lot easier, just start buying a nicer suit.

---

[2] Probably not a Kardashian.

Grooming is one part of this. You need to look professional in all aspects.

Every time you communicate, in email, on the phone, in person, step up your game. Especially when you write something. Make it look good. Make it something your mum would be proud of. Don't have simple spelling mistakes or bad grammar in emails. Don't half ass a presentation. Go the extra mile and put some company logos and themes on that PowerPoint or report. Put some basic formatting on that Excel table. Like putting on a tie. Step things up a notch.

Ask yourself, does the thing you are producing look professional. Your IT systems are probably professional. You do things to a high standard and boast to your IT friends. Therefore, make everything you do like that.

Club Rule 2: Talk the Talk

In the IT department, discussions are usually centred around things IT people like to do. Whether it's Game of Thrones, or streaming services and shows or the latest in tech news and innovation.

In the Executive Club, there's discussion that's entirely different but central to the focus of the group. It's company performance and results, business news, finance news.

This is a discussion you need to learn how to have. The good news, as an IT person, you probably already have a great handle on the company overall and what each department does and what KPIs and outcomes executives are interested in. IT people fix everyone's computer and if you are paying attention you should know what's important for each section of the business.

You might have got one up on someone who is stuck in one location daily.

Do you keep up with business news? Is the stock market going up or down? Are there interesting mergers and acquisitions that people are talking about? Is it time to invest in Gold[3]?

These are things that the Executive Club will totally be talking about. And you need to be part of the conversation and follow along. They follow these things for the same reason we read Slashdot and tech news sites. They keep us in the wider loop, tell us what's going on and watching how others handle situations helps those who are watching valuable lessons to either make them rich, or keep them from looking stupid.

Start reading business news. Begin to learn concepts about running companies that you don't know about. What is a company valuation and why is it important? Learn more about IPOs and shares. How and why companies report to the market. What those documents and announcements say and how you interpret them.

---

[3] General rule of Gold investment: If stock market is bad then yes. If it's good, then no.

These are the things that you learn by going to Business School and getting an MBA. But they aren't some super-secret subject the smarter than average prospective CIO can't learn.

If you're trying to get into the club you need to start seeing businesses from this perspective. As you do you can start to do business from this perspective. You can step out from your IT world, to view things with a wider lens.

Club Rule 3: Act with Authority

As you become more senior in a company, either through direct promotion or time in a role, you will start to have some level of authority within a business. Within IT departments, this initially will usually be authority over certain systems, say responsibility for backups or monitoring systems, or ownership for a specific customer if you're part of an MSP.

At some point, this may be some level of seniority over your colleagues by virtual of your age, experience etc.

And it's about time right! You've earned a bit of authority and respect. Those young kids should call you sir and get off your lawn. They've no idea how good they've had it. Back in my day……

You've always had responsibility but now you are getting authority to go with it.

This is the difficult 2nd album, the final act to bring your play to a conclusion, the most difficult part of the trifecta to complete. This is where the lines become blurry and grey, and the answers not so easy to come by.

If you're ready for membership into the club you need to start acting with authority.

This means you need to make sure you are using your authority (however much of it you have), to ensure you're meeting your continuingly expanding responsibility.

It is easy to work when everyone's behaving and all following the rules. But how do you go about correcting your team when they step outside how they should be acting? How do you correct other employees outside your own team, or even more difficult how do you deal with other colleagues?

There is no technology to fall back on here, it's all people skills. Do you act with grace and poise, effortlessly dealing with people, commanding quiet respect as you quietly resolve problems throughout the day? Or do you stomp through the workplace leaving a trail of resentment and antipathy?

Some days you'll be as smooth as Jon Luc Picard, ever in command and control, wowing people with your calm but firm managing of day-to-day issues. Otherwise, you'll be Obadiah Staine shouting, *"Tony Stark built this in a cave, from a box of scraps!"*

I use fake examples because in the real world nobody ever gets it 100% right. How you balance every day shows to those in this executive club whether you're ready to take place there or not.

Some of this can sound like I'm just trying to *My Fair Lady*[4] you into management. It's a tale as old as time. Take the quiet nerdy girl, let down her hair from its untidy bun, remove her glass and boom Wow she's stunning!

As you might have guessed, there are a few parts to it.

Firstly, you are actively trying to interview for a position by turning up every day and acting like you can do the role.

Every day you show up for work is an interview for that next promotion. And remember our golden rule, nobody knows what you do. Mostly, people just assume you're competent anyways, so looking, sounding, and acting like it are all there to reinforce just how good you are.

More importantly, those who are not looking, sounding and acting the part, are actively showing they are definitely not part of the club. Even if they want in.

Maybe you're too cool for this school. Too bad, this school is private and membership is earned.

---

[4] Pygmalion if you are a fan of the stage over film

Secondly, part of this is learning. You have IT skills, but you don't necessarily have all the business skills. So actively learning about companies from the top end of things is your training. To not just appear to be ready for club membership but proving that you are earning your membership to it. Once you start acting with authority, you know how to use it effectively when you are given more and more of it.

This ultimately is an exercise in becoming more professional, more executive. Becoming someone who's ready for senior leadership of a company. How and what that looks like for you is something that you will develop over time. It's certainly more than putting on a fancy suit, or spouting random stock market bets, or being a jerk to people just because you outrank them.

It is certainly different from that guy who started his career resetting passwords and managing ticket queues. That used to be your life, now it's evolving.

Are you ready to start stepping into the executive club? Maybe you realise you aren't cut out for it. This is a great thing to realise. Not everyone is the CEO or CIO of Fortune 500 companies. It's not an easy job and it's not for everyone.

I encourage everyone I work with to always be creating a long-term plan around their career. Look to where you want to be in 5–10 years. Everyone has different ideas.

Some people have quite lofty goals. They want to be CIO in 5 years, and they are 19 now. That's going to be a meteoric rise but sure let's map out what that looks like.

Some people are happy where they are. This is fine. But I encourage everyone to look at how they can always be growing as an individual.

Most people are probably in between this. We have goals, to some reasonable-ish level, with or without a plan on how to achieve them.

A lot of times people find what they thought they wanted isn't actually what they want. IT people find managing people nowhere near as fulfilling as managing technology (remember how we love a+b=c), and so the goal changes.

We are all people[5] and these are all reasonable and understandable situations to find yourself in. It's always better to realise a problem in your career earlier than later, so you can correct it.

Self-reflection is the most important part of the process. Along with being harshly honest with yourself. A surprising discovery for me was that I hated working solely on technology by myself. I NEED people around. I thrive in an environment where I have colleagues around me on a day-to-day basis. That was a game changing revelation. I'm a people person? I like working in teams? Who knew?

_____

[5] Citation needed

These things can take far longer to find out[6], and usually only happen after spending the time in different working environments to know.

Continual self-reflection, being completely honest with yourself is the only way to understand what the right path is for you. Having a mentor, manager or colleague who can help discuss things with you is super helpful in this process.

---

[6] It took me a decade or more

How to make people care about IT

Back to our core problem *"**Nobody knows what you do, and nobody cares**"*

It's time to come back and face this problem. Ties are optional in this chapter.

Whatever your role is in an organisation, within the IT department you need to step up to and address this issue.

Whether you are the CIO/Director/IT Manager/Top Dog or the newest, greenest 1st level helpdesk, pimply faced youth[1] there is, you need to be part of the solution.

---

[1] aka PFY

Because the truth is IT departments are highly valuable. But they are mostly undervalued[2].

We can be the source of massive improvements within an organisation, but usually, we are overlooked.

I'm pretty sure you are sick of being undervalued, overlooked and under-appreciated. You want to be more than just a guy who resets passwords and checks backups. Your true value is in business improvement, continuous improvement, things like digital transformations and deriving value from all that data you manage.

If your IT team is just a cost centre hanging off the finance department, then it's time to make some changes.

It hurts to hear that "people don't care"

I always hear IT people playing tough.

> *"I don't care what all these stupid people think, I come into the office and work faster, smarter and harder than entire departments. I'm way more important than other people, I could shut down the whole system"*

---

[2] Jurassic World would still be around if hired more than just one IT guy

Hold up there tough guy. You think you sound tough, but you end up sounding like Milton Waddoms

> *Excuse me you took my red Swingline stapler. I told them if they moved my desk one more time I'm going to burn the whole place down!*

We have a bit of an inferiority complex. You could shut down the email system and everyone would cry, but the payroll officer could just not pay everyone for a week and people would be far more upset. Everyone has some level of responsibility, we get it.

The subtext I hear in these rants is:

I get respect from my IT colleagues; I should get it from the entire company too

Sure, you work mildly hard most days, with some sneaky web browsing in the afternoon when your brain is a little fried. You get calls out of hours and make changes on a Friday night. It's cool but you're no saint and you're hardly changing the world.

One golden rule exists within IT that even IT people don't recognise.

Respect is our currency

IT people have a currency of respect not just within their own teams, or company but through the entire IT industry. It's based on the simple idea that the better we are at our jobs the more respect we earn.

Are you a PowerShell God who can automate even the coffee maker? *Respect!*

Are you a Linux guy who builds his own custom kernel for that extra performance? *Respect!*

Do you help your colleagues when they need it? *Respect!*

Do you share knowledge with your team? *Respect!*

Are you just a damn good sysadmin? *Respect!*

Did you invent the Apple 1 and 2? **Much Respect Woz!**

Are you a crazy old guy ranting about free software? **No respect crazy Richard Stallman!**

There are no Oscars for sysadmins or Emmys for programmers. We don't want a trophy or a stupid plaque. We don't want you to stand us up in front of the entire company for an empty handshake with the CEO. Does he know how much freaking Java you wrote? No. Do those regular employees know how many IOPS you gained out of the aging storage systems? They can't even spell IOPs[3].

But will you be pissed if you don't have that respect from your peers? Hell yes.

---

[3] I cant even remember what it stands for before a coffee or two

IT people only want two things. Respect and bonus cheques.

That's why there are stories of admiration about that guy who fixed a network router by routing packets through a custom Linux VM on his laptop for a few hours as a hack. For all of LA[4].

Or conversely, the story about the guy who programmed his section of the application in Delphi because Pascal is the one and only true language and .Net is just a passing phase. What! Why would you do such a thing!

It works both ways. You can earn it and lose it. But we are strangely loyal to our colleagues when they do earn our respect. I imagine that's why Reddit works on up and down votes. You either get respect or not. It's why you can be technically extremely proficient, but also a massive asshole. The Dr House theory. We respect the technical proficiency and overlook being a jerk.

But here's the big catch.

Most other places don't run on the currency of respect. Most places run on the good old chain o' command.

So, you can be a massive jerk, but nobody outside of the IT team will talk to you. You can be much less of a jerk and just socially awkward but great

_____

[4] I heard something like this actually happened. Respect!

at awk (and sed and grep), and nobody will talk to you.

They will respect their boss even though they are completely incompetent when everyone in IT sees right through their façade.

Hence the issue. Non-IT personnel don't have the tech skills to recognise your l33t hacker skills and thus you can't earn their respect.

Even more, if you are a massive Dr House style asshole, and save bytes and not lives, nobody will care, and they will just treat you like you're a massive asshole[5].

What we discover is a massive disconnect between the way IT teams work and the way most other teams work. I'm slightly generalising as I imagine other specialty teams probably work like this. Two that come to mind are Doctors (time travellers and humans) and Consulting Detectives.

I personally like that we work in respect in some ways. It allows the truly talented to be recognised, and over time go from simply colleagues to slowly becoming IT mythology.

Where do we go from here? Do we tear this down and start again? It's pretty much impossible as we are all entirely too stubborn for that[6]. Along with the fact it's pretty much hardwired into our brains.

---

[5] Which is how House was treated by most people anyways.
[6] Most wives, including mine, would agree

They say self-awareness (I think therefore I am) is the first step to enlightenment so understanding ourselves is the first of an undetermined number of steps. The second step is therefore next.

The next step is communication

After our brief encounter with enlightenment, we need to get back to the matter of teaching people what we do and why we are important.

The easiest and most obvious way of making people care about IT is to start turning off circuit breakers in server rooms and pressing big red buttons in the data centre.

It's bold and mostly likely extremely effective. Unfortunately, however memorable it would be, it still doesn't solve the first part of the issue.

Let me go back to the first chapter. IT people. We are not by our nature extremely good at walking around saying how great we are. We are generally pretty good at what we do.

Ask any IT department, the project always fails due to bad managers, or project managers or budget problems. Anything but the technicians themselves. Except when there is a lack of technicians.

Communication is potentially the key here.

As an IT technician, you are by definition a "keyboard warrior". Work is done at the keyboard, preferably mechanical, in front of 2 to 3 screens. Productivity is exclusively defined by keystrokes and mouse clicks. If this decreases so does the work getting done.

This is not entirely the case.

Think about it. You've been hard at work slogging on that keyboard for years. Does it make the communication any better? No.

So logically, you need a change of approach. You need a new function. Part of your routine needs to involve engaging colleagues and doing two things:

- Learning more about what they do and how they do it
- Making them aware of what you do and how it impacts them

This is entirely an informal process. But it is entirely active process. You need to go find people to talk to. Talking to them when they come to tell you about something that is broken is not enough.

My tip for people is to spend more time in the lunchroom. It sounds entirely counter-intuitive but hear me out.

Go drink more water, coffee, tea, or whatever, anything that puts you in a common area like your lunchroom with people. If there's people there, you can if you're courageous enough, actually talk to them.

Sounds crazy! But wait, hear me out.

Start to be where people are and start to have something work-related to talk about. When you get asked "*how's things?*" you say more than "*fine thanks*".

There are endless responses available. You're always going to be working on a project or fixing something, so start with that. Always make it positive. Projects are good because they are usually something new, or an upgrade or improvement. You don't need to say much, just a few words about it.

Things I like to chat about:

- Projects are a great start. They are usually positive and show things are (hopefully) improving
- Talking about regular maintenance can sound boring but shows you care about key systems. "You look tired", "Oh yeah I was up late doing <maintenance> on <system x> to make it better.". Reinforce things like "we do that once a month to help keep it running smooth"
- Ask someone a soft ball question about a system you know you will get a positive response about "Hey how's your new PC running?" "how's <system x> going now we've upgraded? Have you noticed an improvement?"

It may sound dumb, but you're engaging colleagues in IT discussions, subtly (hopefully) getting feedback, and letting them know what you're doing day to day. Keep the technical details brief cause nobody cares; you're highlighting the fact that you care about something they use.

Because people don't know specifics about IT you can make it sound a little more grandiose than it might be. Just be careful you don't try and oversell it too much.

"I spent all night recalibrating the router to adjust for upcoming solar activity"

Yeah, nobody's buying that one.

Not every conversation has to be an opportunity to sell your IT department or job. You're not someone trapped in a pyramid scheme with $10,000 worth of product in the garage to move. You're more like the Tupperware mums. Of course, you're having a party soon and could totally host one for you if you'd like, but you also love to show people photos of your kids too. You have more than one thing.

> As a manager your instinct is probably to stay the same keyboard warrior with a few more meetings in the schedule. However, the phone is going to be your most valuable tool on your desk and going to meetings key to ensuring people are aware of your team and what you are doing.

This whole concept of talking to people about what you're working on, works for meetings too. Most tech people hate meetings, but they are an excellent way of highlighting what you do. If you have a chance in a regular meeting to contribute, make sure you have thought about what you will say, make notes, for heaven's sake update any meeting minutes before you go in, and keep things interesting as possible. People make jokes in eulogies so you can make your weekly meetings fun too.

What do you discuss in meetings? Well, here are some more ideas.

Your latest telecommunications contract may take 6 months to negotiate. Do users get better internet? Yes, then let them know how hard you're working on it. Just turning the dial up on the internet and not telling anyone means two things.

1. Most people won't even notice that you increased the speeds.
2. Internet upgrades are never just a 5-minute thing.

Planning a desktop refresh for a department or location? By goodness let them know how great it will be!

Remember, nobody knows that you are doing these things. You need to tell them. When you do things that provide direct value to end users, all the better. How great is that new computer going to be? A million times better than the crap $500 one they just bought for home? Yes? Then make sure they know this.

People will respond to this. People love to show off a little and one up their friends.

*Our work just got 100Mb internet
connection! That's nothing, we just got
100Gig*

Sounds small, sounds petty, but it's important.
Plus, people love to be petty[7] so why not give them
a reason to be.

Something else to consider is how you
communicate outages to your group. I know in the
past I've skulked around waiting until nobody is on
the system to reboot that system or make a small
change to have the least effect on people.

Start to communicate all your changes. Have a
great looking email template, or intranet
announcement and make sure people have some
way of knowing that the IT team is working hard
late at night, on a weekend, so that systems are
working for them.

They may not read the email; they may not
understand the technical details of what the
change is. But that's not entirely the point. You
always want to give your employees notice of an
outage, and as a side-effect, show that you are
doing upgrades or maintenance or something that
is proactive to the system.

This helps to change the narrative, of not knowing
what the IT department does, to at least one

---

[7] I mean we could work on not being petty but it's
kind of fun

where employees are shown that the IT team is well thought out, proactive and professional.

That hopefully change the initial reaction from one of *"what do we pay these people for"* to something more productive.

This is key because until people start to have a more positive response to IT within the company you can't move on to work with them more effectively.

Water cooler talk is a great start. Change management notifications a great idea as well. But you need more. I would encourage teams to sit down together, work out a communications strategy for your team. To whom do you communicate? When do you do it? What forms does it take?

Have a strategy around communication, review it regularly. Get feedback from key people outside the team. Outside of IT entirely.

Friends outside of IT? Yeah, you're going to need to find some of those….

How to Manage IT personnel

The long-awaited definitive guide

For most of your career you've been managing technology. Those fast, dumb computers we love so much. You set a config on a Cisco router and it will route packets until the zombie apocalypse, or until it loses power reboots and reverts to the saved config, because you didn't do a **copy run start.** That's the beauty and predictability of IT. I've come back to companies 10 years later to be told that a script I wrote back then is still running on the same server. Computers are nothing but predictable.

People on the other hand are nothing like computers. Even the people who seem like they are in fact an android in hiding are not.

To make it worse the people that you work with every day are nothing like the people in all the other departments. See my first chapter. We are different. Our brains are wired differently.

So do two big things for me.

Stop trying to manage your IT team like computers

Stop trying to manage your IT team like everyone else

If you approach your management of people differently for your IT team then everyone is going to have a better time.

People hate change, but what do IT people hate?

Most people hate it when IT people change things. They were happy on Windows XP, then you made them switch to Win 7. Then you made them upgrade to Windows 10. Why? They were happy on XP or Win 7 or on DOS 6.2. Technical change is difficult for a lot of people. They fear that they will be caught out and their lack of IT skills uncovered. They can fear this so much that any benefit of change can be lost.

A lot of people just like to come to work, do the process and then leave. There's nothing more than that. Their lives are outside of the 9-5 hours. Work + Time = Money. Money fuels life outside of work. People have done this for generations. 30 years of the same repetitive tasks on the same set of machines. Come in, check out the brain, use it later. Now the same types of people try and do this at a desk with a computer and attempt the same.

What do we do for these people? Change stuff all the time! Well, the bad news is that these people are going to have to cope. Hardware breaks or needs replacement. Operating systems come and go. Times change and we all must deal with it.

We will look at managing change with end users later, but for now, just contrast this with how IT people see change.

IT people, we see the technical benefits right away. New PC is faster, new switch is 40Gb not 10Gb, more disk, better software, less bugs, etc. We aren't afraid of the technology and so we can embrace that change. That change is going to include teething problems, or out of hours work, but we don't care. It's a chance for learning, gaining experience in new technology, realising the benefits of something new.

IT people don't like sitting on old equipment or software and watching the world pass them by, for no good reason. IT is a fast-moving industry. Things last 3-5 years. Hardware, software, Operating Systems. There's very little chance to sit and enjoy the fruits of our labour before the next wave of change happens.

For the most part, we love this. If we stay still for too long, we feel like ants are crawling under our skin and we have to move. Move systems, move jobs, move industries. Every day we see that change around us, in the industry news, with our colleagues, with vendors and like a surfer, we want to be riding that wave. It's what helps draw us into the industry.

There are exceptions to this. But 99 times out of 100, if you drop some new hardware on the desk of an IT guy, it's going to be installed by the end of the day.

Ok, so we love change.

Here's a test though. Tell everyone in your team that you're going to sit them all at different desks, or even worse, tell everyone you're moving to hot desks, and they get a new desk every day. I bet you get a different reaction to the infrastructure changes.

We love change, but can't take a dose of our own medicine?

No, not quite. People love being within a comfort zone. Pushing anyone out of their comfort zone is going to be difficult. Comfort zones are different for everyone. Technology changes. No problem. But start to change other things, desks, teams, process, then you start to find things more difficult.

One time when I was much younger, as a joke, someone in my call centre team turned the motivation posters upside down. Senior management freaked out and there were a lot of meetings and hushed discussions around this alteration. It was like we'd hung the national flag upside down during a coup of the country. Apparently, those motivational posters were in fact a key management tool in motivating "the team" [1]. The guy who did it thought it was mildly amusing at best, and that nobody would notice until a least lunch time. At which point posters would be hung the right way and people would continue with their lives. Boy was he wrong. If I remember correctly, he even got a promotion in that company later on.

People have a maximum level

As I get older and watch my friends around me grow and develop, it's easier as we get well into our lives to see that not everyone is at the same level. A lot of my friends are married and have kids. Some of my friends have purchased houses in the "competitive" Sydney market, others are still renting. Some friends are running small businesses, some manage teams of people, others are experts in specific fields, and others have a job, but not a career.

Let's be really clear for any friends I have left; I love them all. The position in life they are at now

---

[1] "If we don't look after the customer someone else will" more like "if I don't get a pay rise soon someone will...give me one...when I move to a better job". That one needs a bigger poster though.

doesn't determine what their maximum competency in a specific area is or will be.

However, when I look at people in their workplaces, I see people with varied levels of potential. It's a tricky thing potential. We are told when we are young there is an unlimited supply of potential. But that's probably a lie. It's not a simple as unlocking some hidden chest labelled potential and letting it flow out of us until we have hit super star-dome.

Potential is more like our ability to multiple our natural ability, plus intelligence (in all forms) put that together with as much knowledge, experience as we can gather. In a formula it probably looks like this:

$$P = NA \times (IQ + EQ) + K + EXP$$

Maths was never really my strong suit, but you could probably argue whether there are multipliers for any of these factors and which have more importance.

Does Knowledge and EXPerience count for everything…. sadly no.

But this merely is an indicator of potential. How we use this potential in our actual lives is based on a bunch of factors that include the types of opportunities we get, what kind of start we have in life, and the actual amount of hard work we put in.

Anyone who is vaguely successful in life will of course put their success down to high potential and hard work. But inside they thank their lucky stars for that great boss they once had, or the job interview they aced that got them out of a terrible spot onto a great career. Hard work is super important. Having a high potential is super important. But being lucky helps. Think about all the terrible bosses you've worked for who got their job because they went to the right school, knew the right people, were born into the right family. Look at all the talented people who never got that break to make it big.

More than that, look at all the people who never hustled, pushed, fought their way to be in the right spot at the right time. You, in a lot of ways, make your own luck.

So many people never try and so, they never achieve. Some people ensure they use all the ability they have, to get to the right spot in their career, with the right attitude, to meet the right people to help them rise up to the next level in life.

Take a look around your IT department. You have people at various stages of their career, various levels of potential and different attitudes. Some colleagues make you excited to come to work. Others may make you sigh a lot.

The exciting part is YOU are the person who will help those colleagues.

Good leaders help those that are willing to get to the next step in their career.

Great leaders help everyone to be better.

I really hope you want to be a great leader. To help make everyone around you to be the best of themselves.

Not everyone is destined for career greatness. We are not all going to become the next Bill Gates, Steve Wozniak, Linus Torvalds, or Satya Nadella. It's just not reality. But what we can ALL do is become the best version of ourselves. The best some of my colleagues past and present could be is equally as important as any of the great IT leaders and innovators.

You don't start by changing the world for everyone, you start by change one person's world. At the end of your career if you keep changing the world for just one person at a time you may be surprised just how much you've influenced it.

People aren't computers

L arge scale IT projects are failing every day in the most public and spectacular way. Pick any number of government run websites around the world and you get an endless list of terribly implemented projects which are horrible at best and abandoned at worst.

For all the money and oversight and resources thrown at these projects, why do they still fail? Have we not learnt the secret to success yet?

I think that the problem always comes down to people.

We underestimate the number of people we need for a project, but particularly how much individuals contribute personally to an IT project.

Roads and bridges are easier. The vision is easily communicated. The plans are readily available, easily understood and the whole thing can be broken down into pieces. Literally, pieces of the bridge are delivered and put together. The road has a specific plan. Specific tools and machines that people can drive to accomplish the task. Digging a tunnel? Get a team on that tunnel boring machine and keep those meters going.

But IT projects can be difficult. Putting together hardware can be easy enough. Get it designed, costed, quoted by vendors, and start racking things together in the data centre. But once you get to the software, the website, the design, things get tricky.

Are 1000 programmers better than 1? Probably only if there an easily communicated predetermined plan.

Is there a lone software architect trying to design a system that has constant project scope creep? What happens when that guy is sick for a day, or two or a month? How long does it take to pick up a large software project and get up to speed with it? I know myself for a new infrastructure environment I always feel it takes around 6 months to really get a handle on it. That's for something small under 1000 seat type organisation. A lot of people would call that small business.

I think this is the key to these types of projects. Key people hold it together because they hold the keys to the kingdom. Not necessarily because they want to. Mostly out of necessity. Nobody else can hold together so many distinct, rapidly change pieces. Inevitably at some point, there was documentation, a database schema, software class definitions, but they are so obsolete as to make them merely a shadow what exists now.

The documentation could be updated, but there are deadlines and code and changes to manage.

I'm sure somewhere in all of this is a project manager with a Gantt chart that has a poor software engineer working 9-5, 5 days a week every day for 6months. Assuming a static number of lines per day are written. Then we multiply it by 10. 10 software engineers, pushing out code a rate of x lines per day. Or whatever metric you want to choose.

The reality of what those 10 coders do on any one day is never going to look like that Gantt chart on any single day…..ever. Between a sick day here or there, to ducking out early to pick the kids up to school, to weekly meetings, daily stand ups, company morning teas.

A day of purely no inspiration, or endless errors that can't be found. A few hours to do a knowledge transfer, from one piece of the project to another. Writing a library that's never used. Writing code that is out of date when the spec is changed every day for 2 weeks as nobody can agree.

Software engineers are not computers. You can't have them writing code in shifts, one taking over from the other 3 shifts 8 hours at a time. People are squishy, sensitive beings. They need sleep, and nourishment and importantly caffeine. They are late, or uninspired, or distracted, or vary their productivity (however, you measure it), in a million different ways. Each one of them works efficiently in different ways. Some of them like putting on headphones and not looking up for 12 hours straight. Some need constant validation; most hate being put up in front of the team let alone entire companies and showered with praise.

This is the crux of working with people. They are all different. IT people are different from other teams, but within that subset, we are wildly different ourselves.

What makes us happy and productive is different between individuals and may change for no apparent reason.

This is why managing people can such a hard job. There are no easy answers I can give you to solve all your personnel problems.

However, there are some suggestions. You need to understand how each of your team works. How to get the best out of them. The easiest way is to listen to them, actually sit down and talk with them. Ask them how they are feeling, how they prefer to be managed. A lot of people won't actually know what the answer is for them. But in all honesty, nobody may have ever asked them.

I always think about the bosses I thought were the best and then why I thought they were great. Clearly, a boss who shouts and treats you like crap is not going to be one you enjoy working for. But it's more than just being nice. I'd suggest there are 4 things:

1. Does a manager spend time talking to you explaining their vision clearly? As an employee, once I understand what the overall aim/goal/vision/mission is at any level, I immediately can understand what my role should be. What I should be focusing on, what I should be worried about. Once I understand the vision I can start working independently, effectively, autonomously, and purposely.

2. Does a manager spend time listening to you? I want to be listened to, to feel like my ideas, thoughts and feedback is important. This is especially true in IT; we are all about ideas. We only really deal in ideas, and occasionally hardware. Some industries you can drive past a building or over a bridge or see a tower, and someone can say "I built that". It's tangible, relatable. But in IT we mostly build concepts. We change 1s to 0s and 0s to 1s in a very specific order and it makes electrons move in a certain way. That's why remodelling your server room or datacentre, or network closet always seems that little bit more satisfying. You can point to that and say "I did that" to people and they get it. Point to a bunch of code and it's not the same. So being able to contribute even just feedback or your feelings about something is critical. Do you have trust? Does your manager trust you to work with some level of autonomy?

3. Can you make mistakes? Are you in fear of getting something wrong, feeling like you've

got a noose around your head ready to be fired for any little thing that goes wrong? Or do you have confidence that your manager has your back. That there's a level of understanding that sometimes even with the greatest of care, things can still go wrong. Nobody likes feeling like they are one mistake away from unemployment. Conversely, do you get told when you do a great job?

4. Do you have respect? IT runs on respect. You need it from your manager. Even if they are not technical.

5. Are you valued? Even the lowest helpdesk jockey needs to feel the love. There's always someone who's more qualified or more experienced than you in IT, but are you valued for your contribution. Nobody is the best, but we all can bring value to the workplace, even if it's just getting the job done as best we can, with a friendly attitude along the way.

If you have all those things as an employee, hopefully, you're feeling pretty great about your job. As a manager, if you can accomplish this with your direct reports then you're doing great. The great trick is how to do this for everyone. Everyone is going to need a customized response.

Service Catalogues

Why you need them

Most organisations that implement ITIL in any way are always quick to get a ticketing system in place. Incidents and Service Requests and even some form of Change Management. A good ticketing system is indeed a foundational tool for an IT department.

Like all great IT people, we all have a sense of how ITIL works, some better than others. However, the absolute bedrock of a ticketing system and the entire IT department is a working Service Catalogue.

Do you have one? Have you read it? Has anyone else read it?

If you answered 3 from 3 then good for you! But I'm guessing that could be less than one percent of you can say that.

Service Catalogues are not the most interesting of documents. They don't have amusing stories or pretty pictures. However, a Service Catalogue is the **most** important and powerful document in your world.

A Service Catalogue is a document that defines the services that you as an IT department provide to an organisation. It includes each service and details around the support you provide. The What, When, How and Why of supporting each service.

But the kicker. This document is not just for you. Think of it as a contract between you and the business. What's more, your senior management group[1] will have signed off on this document.

If you do not have a Service Catalogue, this can sound all very formal and difficult. But remember the upside. This is a contract between IT and the business about what you support. But importantly it also defines what you do not support.

This is why these documents are critical. They address the fundamental problem we have been addressing. People who read this document now understand what you do. Ok, maybe they don't fully understand, but there's a marker laid down in a document. It's a stretch to think that everyone in a business will read this document. But that's ok.

---

[1] IT Governance team. You have one, right? We'll get to that.

Think of this as a contract. It's a contract between the IT department and the business. This might be a process where you need to guide people through a whole lot of it. Drag them kicking and screaming as it were[2]. But the guidance and the negotiation of this document is super important.

Take a basic service like email. A CIO I know negotiated a service catalogue with the IT governance team which was essentially the CEO and CFO[3]. They of course want 100% uptime in their email system.

   "Email absolutely can't be down!"

The CIO responds: *"we can definitely do that. However, right now we promise you 99.9% uptime. To do this we have some redundancy, no out of hours helpdesk, just on call. This works pretty well"*

"However, to guarantee you that extra 0.1% we need to make a number of changes. More redundant email servers, 24x7 staffing, etc. It's going to be more expensive. $50-100K for some more servers, a 3 or 4 more IT staff for coverage"

As he starts to tally up the cost, it dawns on the CFO, does the quickest cost benefit analysis ever and agrees that they can probably live with 99.9% uptime.

---

[2] Potentially in a literal sense
[3] This is perfectly fine for a lot of companies

Now it's important to note that as an IT team they didn't just get to 99.9% and turn off the email server for the rest of the month (all 43 mins of it). They internally have the best intentions of the company at heart as well, they want 100%. But, to guarantee that starts to change the way you architect those systems, as well as the way you staff your helpdesks and teams.

Having this conversation is critical as it includes the key stakeholders in the decision-making process. They own this, as much as IT. Plus they get an insight into the process. There's an opportunity for them to understand why that 0.1% is much more expensive. Conversely, there's the benefit of the wider management team owning this decision and defending it when required.

> *"How come email is down this morning? Those IT guys are useless!"*

> *"Well, we made the decision not to get the extra hardware and staff to save costs, so you'll just have to live with it."*

> *"Oh ok CEO"*

In some cases, yeah, you need a higher uptime, or staff ready to take calls and tickets, and the business will pay. These discussions as you sit down with a governance group (it could just be a CFO or owner, doesn't need to be fancy), and discuss their expectations and yours.

In those moments where you have the opportunity with the key stake holders, it's up to you to make sure you are getting this right. Most of the time you need to drive conversation and point out the pros and cons of decisions that are getting made at the time, what the implications are going to be. Because you have this window of opportunity to get this right and set expectations correctly.

It shouldn't be the only time you discuss your Service Catalogue, you should be doing a review in some regularity, bi-annually or yearly for example. But don't waste your opportunity to get senior people to understand your world better. Maybe after a time, you find that a service needs to be rescoped, and that's fine. That outage wasn't acceptable let's do something to fix it.

One of the most important aspects to a Service Catalogue is what is "in scope". Think about all the things you look after in your team. It's easy to get a base list and core IT items like email and file servers should be easy to knock up a scope for. Trust me, those aren't your problem. Think about the edge cases, the software used in departments, the hardware that's not really owned by any one single team. How do you include these things? It's important you refer to them because it's these little items that you inevitably spend your time on. The old 80/20 rule. Right. Email is super easy, you either host it or put it in the cloud. If it's in the cloud, then there's nothing to do except basic management. If it's Exchange on premise, then the same basic management, but you google search that weird event log when you're not sure what to do. Plus, patch it monthly[4]. Sysadmin 101.

Now consider some of the software the different departments use. Does it have a weird server, with an application that has to be running on the desktop? No silent installer for the client? A weird version of Java? Does it use Flash or Internet Explorer 9? Is it written for a 16bit Windows XP subsystem environment? Does it only use one specific fork of awk? We've all had these weird pieces of software. Inevitably we get dumped with this crazy software and left to deal with it.

Service Catalogues are the time to fight back. Sure, you'll work with your crap software, but understand that it's a two-way street.

Is it in the hot DR strategy?

Not with an architecture like that. Sorry, in an emergency you're waiting for backups.

Can you include it with your auto patching setup?

Nope, it's manually getting patched. Yes, our manual patching is done on Tuesday at 2:30 pm. If that's not acceptable, then let's negotiate for some kind of after-hours support.

The reality of life is that sometimes people with no software experience, puke out code[5] that somehow compiles into a system that you are

---

[4] You do patch? right?
[5] 1000 monkeys working for 1000 years eventually make something compile.... except it's in COBOL.

asked to support. Until we can legally imprison these people and maybe cut off their hands to stop it from happening again, it's a fact of life. However, what we can do as a mature IT team, is to document this atrocity and ensure that everyone understands the implications of using it.

On the day the "designers" of the system vomit out another release, which requires everyone to be a local admin and won't be integrated into your perfectly sculptured SCCM or Puppet system because it has no /S on its .bat file of an "installer". When your users demand you install it immediately onto 10,000 of your most finely tuned desktops, you can refer back to your Service Catalogue and point to the place that refers to this abomination of spaghetti code and prophesies this day and proclaims "No! It cannot be done, and you must wait!".

So sayeth the Service Catalogue[6].

Of course, this will probably infuriate whoever came to you with the request. Especially if you say it like that. However, stand your ground. You warned them. People agreed. Very senior people whose last name is on the building was there or at least cc'ed on the emails. You don't make your team stay late. You've already agreed to a course of action, and it doesn't include the IT team filling in for other people's bad choices.

---

[6] Amen. On Friday there were lunchtime beers at the pub, and they all rejoiced.

It does include some proactive planning and hopefully, this is part of a list of legacy systems you are all working together to move away from to another vendor.

Then you can choose the following retirement options for this software:

a) Move it to a farm "upstate"
b) Put it out to stud like a racehorse
c) Flush it down the toilet like a dead goldfish
d) Take it out the back and shoot it like Travis does with his dog "old yeller" when he gets rabies[7]

PS – I really hate badly written software.

While we can all hate bad software, hopefully, you can see that we change the interaction at play. Rather than having bad software forced upon us, we support it on our own terms, with more realistic outcomes. But further than that, we identify it as "bad software" and start to have the conversation about how we get "good software". Now, hopefully, instead of having this software thrust upon us and being expected to "do your job", when said job is nigh on impossible to support, there is some group ownership of this software with a longer-term view for improvement.

This starts to sound like a way more equitable way of dealing with the problem. It's not always a case

---

[7] Old Yeller is apparently a "coming of age" story. You're not a man until you shoot something you love.

of being able to just say a blanket "No" to any and all requests. There's going to be things we have to do in the name of getting business done. Many times, software doesn't have a replacement we can just wait for the next financial year to purchase. We may have to live with it forever. But, sometimes even just identifying the issues, noting down some way of dealing with it, and setting reasonable expectations for upgrades etc is enough to stop those 4:30 pm on a Friday impossible requests from ending up being "IT's problem". It makes it everyone's problem.

So bad software is one thing, we've dealt with that one.....BANG!..... Service Catalogues can help to remove the grey from other areas as well. IT teams commonly have euphemisms like "electron wrangler" to help identify the fact that commonly we are asked to fix anything that has electricity, like a modern day Fonzie who can hit the Jukebox in just the right spot to get it playing tunes[8].

In a lot of organisations, IT people are realistically the only people that can fix the coffee machine, or the TV in the break room or the jukebox. But let's be honest, are those things critical to the function of the business. With the exception of the coffee machine ... no, they most likely aren't.

---

[8] With streaming music it's not about hitting the right spot on the jukebox, but punching the right hole in the firewall. Still worth wearing a leather jacket when you do it though.

Do people expect you to fix them like they are? These are things that need to be included in your Service Catalogue. Sound basic and they are, but if your team looks after them in any way then it's part of your job. Most likely you find a few things that are more critical than a TV. More likely to be things like the TV in the reception area which customers see, or air conditioning system for the building, or alarm security system, or video surveillance systems.

A lot of these systems have electrons and even networking components. But they can be borderline as far as stock standard IT type items.

Maybe, it's more like the video surveillance system that neither IT nor the maintenance department owns. Both have some level of skills to maintain it, but neither have official responsibility for it.

It might be time to step up and take on that system to ensure it's getting looked after. We can be super reluctant to do that because it's another task on the giant pile of tasks we need to do. What if instead of just piling more work onto your team's list, you actually define this in your Service Catalogue. Then as you go through your entire list of responsibilities you can define what air conditioning maintenance looks like (simple call to a guy). Or what it looks like to take on video surveillance systems. That latter could be quite involved and take on further budget costs, capital costs and time for installation, configuration and maintenance.

By doing this, however, you roll things into your planning, so that ancient old phone system gets replaced with a more modern solution. In doing so you might save the company a large chunk of maintenance costs. This type of complaint is common with IT guys. Why do we have that legacy PABX or old security system which stores recordings onto DVDs? It must be expensive to maintain and there are better ways to do it.

Yes, it is expensive, yes there are better methods. Time to put your big boy pants on. Put a business proposal together and help save the company time, money and effort. I can't imagine an executive who would say no to someone stepping up to take on the responsibility and do it better. Remember that the finance guy who rings the PABX guy to change phone numbers around probably hates it as much as you do. He probably understands there's a better way to do things but he wouldn't know how to get there.

Be sane and help the guy out.

What do you Catalogue for your Service

So you know that you need to look after a service, say email, but what do you put in your Service Catalogue under the entry "Email"?

First of all, determine what the scope of the service "Email" includes. You'd probably write things about sending and receiving, filtering, archiving, litigation hold, permissions, forwarding. Standard stuff. What about email clients like Outlook? Does that count? Well possibly, but that may be included in "Software, Desktop Apps" and feature there.

It's up to you but, after defining your service, you need to scope out how you support it. In this case, you may want to include details of a support team structure which includes Exchange architects, not first level support. It's up to you though and each case is different.

You provide email. How do you intend to provide this service? On prem, cloud, some sort of redundancy? You don't need to include IP addresses and server names, but you should have some details as to the basic architecture you are using or intend to use for this service.

This should lead on to DR, backups, and your SLA[9] for your service. SLA for uptime, SLA for response to an issue with the service, a critical issue with service, and Recovery Time Objectives and Recovery Point Objectives.

SLAs can sound like you're being timed like an Olympic runner, but they help to determine factors around staffing levels, backup systems, DR architecture etc.

---

[9] Service Level Agreement for those playing at home

This is the document you want to give you these types of details. The factors here will help determine a lot about your IT team.

They determine the things you drop everything for to go fix. If email is critical to the business (HINT: it's usually not), then when it's broken, you stop and fix it. That could be 24x7. Maybe that's only when business is conducted which is more like 8x5.

This is a critical distinction. If you agree to 8x5 as critical hours, then by definition after hours are a whole different ball game. Now, that might not mean you can just switch off and let everything die until 8 am the next day, but it could possibly mean that for non-critical systems. A system providing software updates could be down for a day and the business keeps on making widgets.

Which by definition means if it breaks at 9 pm and you fix it at 10 am the next day, you could be well within your SLA period. Nothing is critically affected, widgets are still made, life goes on.

This may not be as important for Joe Bloggs the standard user, but for burnt out IT guy, it would be awesome to know that you don't HAVE to fix that system out of hours. Because in all likelihood, you won't get paid for it. You can get an SMS or email informing you that a non-critical system is down, and you can enjoy your downtime knowing that you are within your right to wait until tomorrow to fix it.

Most likely you get an angry phone call from a user at an unrealistically late hour informing you that a system is done, and by the Service Catalogue you are within your rights to say "No" or have no one on your 24-hour helpdesk who can fix the issue, only do limited troubleshooting.

The point is this is the place to define these criteria.

What is this service?

How does it work?

Who supports it?

What happens when it breaks?

How long is the business able to function without it?

Document it, discuss it, negotiate it and agree on it.

Sword and Shield at the same time

By now, I hope you start to understand why Service Catalogues are important. Without them, we can become slaves to everyone's demands. We have no expectations on system design and DR and backups. We might be expected to do anything for anyone at any time.

This is probably at the heart of a lot of the big complaints I see from IT professionals. We are torn from one critical issue to the next. We are a people in demand.

A big one I see is the Executive who wants item X. Say you have all Windows desktops. Executive comes in with new MacBook[10]. Demands to be able to use said MacBook instead of Windows machine. This is a perfect place to refer to your Service Catalogue. Under desktops you clearly specific Windows 10 supplied by vendor X. As this is not in the Service Catalogue, you can do either one of two things.

Firstly, take the opportunity to include MacBooks as part of the Service Catalogue. This could be a good thing. But first, look through your Catalogue, see what services may need to be changed to accommodate MacOS. There may be software that isn't native on the Mac. Ok well, you can run Parallels and put Windows on it. Technically, this solution may fix your issue. But there's a cost. And most likely a user education cost as well. Your users may struggle to understand Virtual Machines. Maybe, there's a cost to upgrade a system for MacOS support. You may need to train more of your helpdesk on how to support MacOS. Maybe you stand firm that only Executive A can have a MacBook and he supports himself and deals with the consequences. Maybe you are in a situation where you need to expand your support

---

[10] Why is it always a MacBook?

to include multiple OSes anyway and this was inevitable.

Either way, this is the chance to revise your Service Catalogue and include all the ramifications, costs, SLAs etc to the document.

You may find that the Executive just likes the look of the Mac and he doesn't want to have to pay extra costs. You definitely want to have all this agreed on before the Executive brings his shiny MacBook to the next big meeting and EVERY Executive now wants a Mac[11].

Before you had a Service Catalogue, these kinds of requests are potentially difficult to shut down. You're just being petty or no fun when you just say no all the time. Instead, now you are demonstrating how changing the end user environment fundamentally shifts how you provide services to the company all with one MacBook. At the very least you have a concrete document you can review and say these systems do or do not work with this new machine. You may find it quite compatible. You may find that systems you have in place to provide compliance reporting, antivirus and other services which protect the company aren't compatible and you have a demonstratable case of "this breaks our compliance".

That may not be too much of a threat if the widgets you make are toys for kids. But if you make highly

---

[11] Can I offer you a fancy Dell 2-in-1, a Lenovo even? Why MacBooks?

classified widgets for ▮▮▮▮▮▮ then that may prompt more of a response.

If you are overruled and Executive MUST have the MacBook, your Service Catalogue exception may be "supported on best efforts only"

Maybe the request isn't a petty one of MacBooks vs Windows. The process is the same though. Suggesting a change to the services IT provides needs to be vetted against the catalogue to understand the impact. Then if everyone is happy changes and inclusions are made.

You have a tool now. It's your sword and a shield in one. It protects you. It can help fight your battles for you.

Putting it all together

Now after some hard work you have a Service Catalogue. It is for now complete. All services you provide to the business are included. Standard IT stuff. Crap software. Slightly not IT stuff. MacBook's and next year Linux[12].

You now have in your hands or on your screen a document that defines IT for your business.

This is fantastic! Now, the real work can begin. Because this document can determine how you put

---

[12] next year is the year of the Linux Desktop. It always is....and yet never is.

together your IT team. IT documents for how you put together your IT systems.

Before you were just guessing, based on gut feeling. Now you have a mandate.

Sounds amazing and it could be. In most cases, you may not feel you have much to change in your team, in your environment. But over time you have a tool you can use. You use this for planning, for budgeting for understanding where and how your team will grow over time.

IT Governance

I'll break out my execu-speak and say, *"let's circle back on something mentioned earlier"*. IT Governance, I mentioned it a bit, but important to stop and discuss this in more detail.

One of the big mistakes I see is IT teams that operate completely siloed from senior management. It can happen everywhere but's it's very common in small to medium businesses with very small IT teams, 1-4 people.

These teams can be dedicated, diligent and in most cases doing a good job. But despite their best effort they always end up struggling.

They usually have complete autonomy over the technology. In lots of ways, they are quite happy. They can choose software and hardware that suits them. They implement internal systems that can be quite effective for them.

However, they usually struggle, in a few key areas:

- They have difficulty enforcing IT policies to the business
- They have difficulties in making meaningful business process changes
- There can be enormous shadow IT which they cannot reign in
- Changes that heavily include technology are planned and, in many cases, implemented without them.

These problems usually stem from an IT team who, are mostly ignored by the business and potentially considered purely a cost centre by the senior leadership.

I met a team like this recently. It had a great group of IT guys who seemed reasonably qualified. But when I asked them about how they interacted with the senior leadership, they were all very sullen and admitted they only got to talk to the General Manager occasionally, and very informally. They clearly knew there was a problem, didn't know how to solve it. When we spoke, it became clear they had great ideas on how to improve the business, but they were unable to effectively sell these improvements because nobody was really listening. IT was just a cost of doing business and the old school owners didn't have any reason to find any more value in their IT team.

The whole scenario was a shame, as the team seemed to be a great one, but without fixing these issues they were going to be treading water.

This situation arises when there are technical IT guys who don't focus enough on leading but on the technology. Usually, because the technological and end user support challenges are so enormous that it's difficult to get a minute in the day to actually reflect on how to address these problems.

It's not 100% the IT team's fault. These IT teams report to someone. That manager also needs to understand that there's a problem. There are plenty of non-technical managers trying really hard to break IT teams away from their keyboards long enough to have some conversations.

As dedicated IT people, most of us usually care too much about running a "great system", to care about anything else. This is admirable but ultimately can harm the business, their career, and the overall IT departments. Usually because once they have had enough of running into the other struggle areas they've had enough and move on to, unfortunately, repeat the whole thing over again.

Even if you have an excellent rapport with your senior management, any informal interaction is just friendly banter.

To really be effective you will need to have formal interaction with senior leadership. There are different ways to achieve this, which, ultimately depend on your company.

What you want to achieve is relatively simple. The core aims should be:

- Regular review of the IT team performance including helpdesk, projects, and budgets
- Bring key decisions to the IT governance team. Large projects, major vendor purchases.
- Discuss and formally agree on IT policies that affect the wider business.
- Ongoing review and modification of Service Catalogue
- Hear and discuss from the business on changes to the business and how IT will work with them on those changes

These aren't regular IT team meetings. This isn't time for discussing Julie from Accounting and her continuous password reset problems. This is your time to sit the senior staff down and get them working with you. Importantly these are where IT decides with the leadership how things will happen.

This is the discussions on Macs in the office, the password policies, how data transits your network, what vendors you will choose. Once they are made then it's not the decision of an IT guy or even an IT director, it's a business decision made with people at the highest levels.

This is the time to discuss DR requirements. What the business expects when you lose power, or the building burns down. It's your job to help make them understand the implications. What does doing nothing cost? How do we keep things running? What does that even look like?

Most of the work is for you as IT leaders. You need to bring a host of issues to this group to inform them, bring solutions and help get agreement. Getting things right here are going to make a lot of your job easier, more effective, and hopefully more enjoyable.

A lot of things won't be difficult, but they need some selling some PT Barnum and acknowledgement. You may already have the best DR out there. You've done the hard work and things are completely redundant, ready to cut to a hot DR within a moment's notice etc. You may not need any decisions on this, but what you may need to do is let everyone else know just how good your DR is.

Remember, nobody knows what you do. At the start of this process, you may just need to spend a lot of time making people aware of all this hard work you have already done. And if this feels a little self-serving, don't be too put off by doing it. Having a great power management system, or DR, or whatever, is a great encouragement and tick of approval for the senior group. They will need to feel some confidence in you. They may just need some good stories to help them look great.

Importantly this is your time to get input from the senior leadership to understand their concerns. It's about ensuring they understand your concerns. Being the responsible, measured, reasonable adults you can come to quick solutions to all your problems.

Ok, it might not be that quick and easy, but it is a forum to start having conversations at a higher level to get a mutually beneficial outcome.

What does that look like? I'd say it sounds like:

"Here is a proposed infrastructure budget plan for the next 5 years, can your review our projections for company growth and expansion, as well as our proposed costs"

"Can you give us some insight to your forecasts for the next 3 years for project X?"

"What new initiatives are coming up in the next 12 months? How will you need IT to assist?"

"IT team has identified 5 new areas for improvement, we want to discuss which ones we think are important and get approval for them"

These are discussions for your governance team. You need input from your leadership. What are they thinking, planning, and considering? They need to hear from you about your ideas, roadmaps, and costs for the future?

Nobody likes surprises. This is your time to discuss what IT budgets look like in the future and plan accordingly. Do you need to move that 3-year refresh to a 4- or 5-year refresh? What risk implications does that have? What savings does it have? Are you prepared to keep that SAN and add grey-market support to it? Or pay for extended Vendor support?

Having that conversation upfront, being prepared with the numbers, the implications shows that your spending may well be justified. But you can't just spend the company's money without a little justification.

More than just budgets, knowing what the leadership team is thinking, planning, and getting in at the ground of those ideas is critical to helping them implement those ideas well from an IT perspective. This is where you can ensure you don't get dumped with a crappy system that was already bought and paid for. This is where you start to get invited to the initial demo meetings, the working parties and help guide everyone to a more successful outcome.

It's also where you can discuss your personnel. If you want to grow by 30% over the next 12 months, then that's going to increase work load on the helpdesk. How do you staff the team to accommodate that? Have that discussion now. You will need those helpdesk guys sooner than later, to start training them getting them familiar with the environment etc.

Is your team overworked? Then this is the time to ensure you are making decisions about that. Informed decisions. Bring data that shows this is not just a knee jerk reaction to some guys that don't like staying past 4:30 pm on a Friday. What are the metrics for IT support staff ratios for your type of business? One IT person for every 100 employees? What don't you know? You absolutely should. Statistics don't prove everything, but there needs to be at least some metric to help base your decision on. Maybe the metric is simply how often do you see IT people parked in the car park still when you go home[1]?

So yeah, maybe that's why we have a higher turnover than other teams.

If you aren't having these conversations, then do you really have your teams back? They don't have to be outright confrontational. Chances are your leadership may not have ever really considered IT staffing levels. It's your opportunity to help educate them.

Standard metrics are one IT guy to every 150 employees. We have 3 guys and 10,000 employees. No wonder their phones are literally on fire from the sheer amount of phone calls.

As you get more comfortable within the group, you want to start having your non-IT leadership guys asking you questions? What is digital transformation? Do we need a CTO? Should we be building an API? Why aren't we in the "cloud"?

Leaders are asking these questions and if they aren't asking you, then they are asking other

_____

[1] It's a trick question, those guys don't even get a parking space.

people. People you potentially don't want to answer those questions.

> *"Hey, my golf buddy is an IT expert and I've hired him to help move us into the cloud. He starts Monday"*

> *"Ah ok, but we are already in the cloud"*

> *"Well, he's going to be here anyways, so let's just get him to work on helping make things 'better'"*

I think that's how IT horror stories begin[2].

You get paid to be the IT expert in your company. Be the authority on IT. Help your leadership to be informed and making smart choices.

Remember all those times you thought your CEO was not that bright? Well now is your opportunity to help educate him. You've got to put your big boy pants on now. You are part of the leadership of the company, and you need to act like one team.

Half of your job might be to help the rest of the senior leadership understand your issues and what you do. Sound frustrating? Well, that's the reality of the job. CEOs, General Managers, Presidents of countries, they don't know everything. They probably don't know about IT departments and

---

[2] It continues when said consultant brings starts talking about this new thing called "li-nux". "It's pretty cutting edge, you guys probably haven't heard of it"

how to manage them. Time to step up and help them. They don't need another snarky IT guy[3], they need a leader who can inform and guide them into ensuring they are making the right decisions and making important plans for the future.

We've gone long past Julie and her password problems. This is about roadmaps, planning, budgets, and improvements. Aligning the company with IT and IT with the company.

It's not going to be perfect the first time around, and it's going to take you stepping up and being a leader to your senior leadership. Taking initiative, producing the research and the plans, and asking the right questions to take the conversation and by extension the company in the right direction.

If it sounds daunting and difficult then you probably understand what I'm saying. This is why you get paid the big bucks as they say. But you're not entirely on your own. You have a team around you that can help.

Your first step is to have these conversations with the team first. What does your team think are the big challenges? What do they think the budgets look like? Do they feel overworked? Why? How do you solve that?

IT teams are never without an opinion on anything. Use that to your advantage and work up from there.

_____

[3] There's plenty of those to go around

At the end of this process, you should have an IT team that is engaged, feeling like they have been consulted and have input. You should conversely have a senior leadership team that feels the same way.

Now, nobody is the enemy per se. You are aligned in your goals and working towards them constructively. It never quite works out that way, and nobody ever quite gets what they want. But even just regular communication from top to bottom in your organisation would be far more constructive and productive than catching your CEO "when he has a minute".

Why IT Is Difficult

Working in IT is hard work. But it's deceptive. I've worked with miners who spend 12 hours a day underground and can go weeks without seeing the sun. Yes, manual labour is physically difficult, I take nothing away from that. But IT is mentally tough. It can also be physically tough, but those days are probably rare for most of us. UPSes can be surprisingly heavy.

It's one of the great misunderstood and unappreciated facts of working in an IT environment. The days can be mega, the mental concentration can be intense.

All of which is part of any job really, but one thing that I think defines IT environments is the constant demand from our end users.

In a probably now slightly dated reference, Jerry asks Newman on an episode of Seinfeld why postmen are renown for coming into a post office and shooting up the place…"going postal". His answer for me is immensely relatable, "Because the mail never stops! Every day there's more!"

For every ticket I've ever worked on, resolved, and closed … there's always another. For every server I've transformed from dilapidated wreck to finely polished highly tuned masterpiece, there's another ready for me to work on. For every piece of code I've written, there's another line to write. For every network rack I've ever cleaned up, it's only a matter of time until it's messy again.

IT is always unfinished and there's always something to do.

In the midst of these jobs, there is the constant end user requests that are duty bound to resolve. They range from the reasonable, to the strange, to the intriguing (how in the world did it ever work!?!). But they mostly sit in the mundane (my account is locked out again!), the dumb, the demanding and the annoying.

And through all the projects, the tasks that require deep concentration and focus is the constant interruption. From users, manager, colleagues and Senior executives (the ones you CAN'T ignore). All of this is enough to drive anyone a little insane, and certainly test the patience of even the best of us.

I'll acknowledge that lifting heavy things is hard. Building a house is tough. Working in a mine can be exhausting. Being covered in dust and grease, in 45 degrees for 12 hours straight would literally[1] kill me. But at least nobody interrupts you while you've got your head stuck inside a giant truck and asks you if you can fix their kids IPAD[2].

What I'm basically saying is while I hate to see physical violence in any forms. I'm genuinely surprised that you don't hear of IT guys going a little crazy. I'd say the tried and tested method of letting out our aggression is a well walked path of passive aggressiveness, intense sarcasm and taking old printers out into a field and smashing them with a baseball bat[3].

The other large factor in the general stress of an IT worker is the invention of the telephone. Once people can reach us whenever they like, was the downfall of the industry. Bring in mobiles and boom, we are entirely contactable at any time for any reason.

While the occasional phone call is entirely reasonable, it can quickly take over. I worked with a guy who literally took a phone call at least once every 5 minutes all day. Every day. People would

---

[1] I really do mean literally not figuratively.
[2] I could be stuck in solitary confinement in a 3rd world prison and still someone would interrupt my pleasant silence with "Oh you're in IT! can you just have a look at something? I'm sure it won't take long".
[3] It's referred to by psychologists as "The Michael Bolton Method", not to be confused by interrogation technique of the same name.

call his mobile to complain they couldn't get through to him.

"I'm actually on another call. You are always on a call. Yes. Yes, I am".

He was extremely helpful, knowledgeable and to his credit and my surprise always friendly and willing to take those calls. Except for the occasional Friday afternoon when the façade would crack slightly, and you could hear the exhaustion in his voice.

I worked with him 15 years ago, and I don't know if he's still working at that same place, but I bet his extension is still getting calls.

While we might try to introduce boundaries, it can be sometimes impossible to escape. The late-night issue might seem like the end of the world to one person yet entirely inconsequential in the grand scheme of things. It also might be the first time that person has called you at 9 pm on a Tuesday, but unbeknownst to them, it's the 25th call you've had this week.

Somehow users can always know when your head just hits the pillow and your about to drift off to sleep. Then BAM! The phone rings.

Setting Boundaries

This is all very nice and all but clearly unsustainable. How do we resolve the problem? We could adopt the old internet advice strategy of finding a new place to work. This is more often than not a stop gap and doesn't actually go anywhere to solving the problem.

Why? Because the issue was our own fault as much as it was the companies.

Therefore, leaving for a new company without addressing your own issues isn't going to help anyone.

However, if we become a little more introspective, look at our own behaviour we may find a healthier way to find some work/life balance.

Creating value with IT

For most organisations there is no real value in infrastructure. Real business value is found in the application space

I have some bad news time for most of you. Time spent in infrastructure does not provide value to businesses. It's foundational, sometimes boring, and only serves to run applications. While everyone loves a fast network or storage systems with high IOPs and no latency, the reality is that most of the hard work in this space is providing no real value.

Before you come at me with pitch forks, let me explain. For 80% or more of businesses, you consolidate on a virtualisation platform of your choice, put some servers in front of storage and bam! You've got core infrastructure.

Now admittedly, this is critical to the business. You can't run the business without the VMs that run on these machines.

However, for the most part, the fact your storage is 100% optimised is of no REAL value to the business. The redundancy you have with dual everything is providing no value.

What do I mean by value? Does that hardware make money for the company? Short answer no, long answer it's about risk management.

A functioning virtual environment does what it needs. It runs servers. Whether it is great, average, or poor, is usually making no fundamental difference to your company.

Redundancy is of little benefit, until a component breaks. What we are really trying to say is that redundancy is risk management or insurance. Without that second power supply, your server keeps running. So why have a second one? Mitigate risk. Insure the company against a potential failure.

Before we keep diving into the bad news, let me deliver what I think IS the value of IT.

Hint – it's applications.

While you might get a major boost to the ego and much satisfaction by making that SAP system start up in an instant, and process database requests by the millions without breaking a sweat, that mostly doesn't make any difference, if the application and processes around it are inefficient.

I've seen people work "hard", who are actually just copying contents of excel spreadsheets, cell by cell (with no copy or paste), into a new excel spreadsheet. Their end of month accounting process was 3 days of manual typing of information. Whether or not the file server saved those excel files in 10 milliseconds or in 10 mins doesn't make ANY difference when the work being done is costing the business thousands per year in salary.

What does make the business more money is implementing systems that improve process, drive more business to the company, improve profit margins.

For IT departments there is a MASSIVE opportunity to use your skills, knowledge, and experience to really make a difference that's felt on the Profit and Loss statement.

Hopefully, this type of process improvement, application optimisation, integration work excites at least some of you as something that is fundamentally interesting. It could be creating APIs for applications to pass information or writing custom apps.

It might be something as simple as being able to lead some process improvements throughout your business. IT departments work across teams, and so see more of the business that most people. Use that knowledge to help improve processes that interact between teams.

Can we declare that infrastructure is worthless and applications are the champions? Not quite. But it's critical to have strong focus on what's important in a larger sense. Why? Well for one it's going to help you align your longer-term goals with those of your non-IT bosses. They are going to care about what's making money and what's costing money.

You must be able to translate IT into a business language. Reframe your conversations. Investment in IT in a certain area will have a return. Mitigating risk in other areas will prevent catastrophic losses.

Remember the tired trope of the hardworking IT guy. Spends all day building redundancies and testing backups.

> *"I'm the most important person in the company! Without me, nothing would work!"*

That's true - in a sense. But IT infrastructure is a job that has a high impact when it goes wrong and low impact when it's done right. Which is important. But so does Payroll and so does the guy cleaning the toilets.

So be careful, because while you think you may be massively heroic, you just look and sound like the Janitor from Scrubs.

Indeed, success at building reliable infrastructure reduces the chance for a major impact on the business. If your hard work means nothing ever fails, or infrastructure faults that have no business impact due to redundancy, then fantastic! You have done a great job. You may have done it with a fraction of nature's resources and a fool for an assistant. Your reward essentially is satisfaction in a job well done and your weekly pay check.

Now, the second and potentially much harder part of your or your manager's job is to make sure people understand the value you have provided. This comes back to previous chapters around selling yourself and your work.

Infrastructure is ultimately an important foundation for building IT systems. However, it is important to ensure what you build is fit for purpose.

NASA builds rockets with triple redundant computers. This is important when your rocket costs $1bn to develop and each launch is $200m or more. But if you just need a basic file server for your SMB office, triple redundancy is most likely overkill.

It's vital when planning for anything in IT to always go back to your service catalogue and ensure that the system you are building, serves the service you've agreed to.

There's plenty of older Exchange documentation for sizing RAID arrays and calculating IOPS. They contain great information around ensuring your required IOPS can be met even through disk failures and RAID rebuilds. This sounds great but ultimately comes at a cost.

We consider normal usage, per user. Then we consider peak load per user. Then we place overhead for growth. After that, we add disks to maintain IOPS during disk failures.

All of a sudden that disk array has doubled in size, cost, and performance.

Vendors will say you MUST have disk array sized for all of these circumstances. Mostly because it makes those vendors a lot more commission. It also ensures that you don't come back and complain that your expensive system doesn't perform as it should.

However, before you get carried away with IOPS and redundancies, keep your service catalogue in mind.

If we take the example of Exchange, let's consider the actual use case or a user. Employee A in Example Company uses email as a tool to CC their managers on conversations, to demonstrate they are working hard, doing the right thing, and being polite even though the recipient has been rude down this email chain. Employee A sends about 5 emails a day, all of them realistically need to be delivered within a 4 hour window. Anything critical can be substituted as a phone call or actually standing up and walking over to another cubicle.

Manager B in Example Company hates receiving emails, as most of them are copies of files that should be saved on the Example Company Document Library. Hence, while they receive 100 emails a day, only about 5% are actionable. Example Company does no direct line of business through email.

Example Company is in a major city, has infrastructure supplied by a major Tier 1 provider with a 4-hour response contract.

Why would they ever need to over spec anything to do with their Exchange storage! Performance as long as it is somewhat reasonable is of no real consequence. Uptime is the major metric and then not even ultimately critical.

So why is the IT guy at Example Company busting his gut over Exchange? Making sure it's backed up, testing a restore every now and again and ensuring it's patched. Boom covered. On to fixing other problems.

Their Service Catalogue should reflect all of these factors and the focus should be on other key issues.

It's easy to get into a bubble and get carried away with IT metrics. Remember who publishes a lot of these recommendations, they are the ones selling the equipment. That 3-year life cycle is great if you're selling equipment, but in reality, most IT equipment sits in a pretty pristine environments at constant humidity and temperature and does its thing.

There are failures in equipment kept in these types of environments, but I'd say that over the last 30 years, IT hardware has become increasingly more reliable, yet we continue to design systems as if they were fragile babies. IBM tested this a few years ago and put servers outside of their data centre in a tent in the car park. After 12 months failure rates were identical to inside.

Your mileage on equipment may vary. Plus, drawing conclusions from one group of servers in one car park makes statisticians shiver. However, if that teaches us anything, it's us that servers are potentially[1] more resilient than we thought and that the biggest impacts are more likely going to be from other factors.

And so, I present to you without providing any conclusive proof, in increasing levels of risk, the 3 biggest points of failure in your network:

3 – Power issues

Power is a factor outside our control. We act like it isn't, with our UPSes and generators. Every datacentre I've ever been to has told me they have exclusive deals for being first to get more diesel when that big apocalypse comes. But if everyone is top of the list then surely someone misses out.

Even if you can power your server room with a tidy generator with a massive supply of diesel to last the zombie apocalypse, that's useless if the rest of the building has no power. At least your uptimes aren't affected[2].

---

[1] Words like "potentially" gives wiggle room to drawing conclusions on poor sample sizes and helps calm those statisticians down. Also bring them hot tea.
[2] Though long uptimes equal unpatched and vulnerable systems

2 – Internet outages

Nothing kills the internet like a backhoe through a fibre optic cable. While we are on the cusp of 5G internet, it's not wireless everywhere, it's got to go to a cable somewhere. You might just find that your internet and backup mobile connection terminate in the exact same place …. downstream of the backhoe.

While the internet is amazing and not susceptible to things like single fibre optics breaking whole swathes of connections. It does. And when it does I just know some network guy is saying to his bosses "hey you know that upgrade project we didn't do…."

1 – Human error

You can't escape people doing dumb things. Even this week I accidentally deleted a disk on a production server. I was confused, tired and rushing[3]. I'm an IT professional with over 20 years' experience, breaking things on multiple continents[4]. Imagine what an untrained person could do. Imagine what I could do if I used my powers for evil and not for good.

---

[3] Luckily our backups were solid and things were quickly restored

[4] Let me get my hands on one of those rovers on Mars, make me galactic

You can automate processes and reduce the risk of people doing dumb things, but even the best of us makes mistakes.

Users will continue to make mistakes, break things, find new ways of breaking things and generally make a mess of our best laid plans while stomping around like overgrown children.

Managers will do their best. When they are presented with all the facts they will decide based on their own prejudices and biases ie, a stupid one.

These are the worst cases of stupid, but you can't avoid them completely. This is why Human Error is number 1 on our list and will be every year until the robots uprising[5].

Bottom line, some failures we just can't avoid. Some we can, but the reality of the situation means that the cost of solving the potential impact is more than what the business is willing to pay. At the end of the day that might be the right call.

We inherently want our IT systems to be unstoppable, and a quiet, dark server room with no fans whirring and no flashy lights is the most unnerving place for any good sysadmin to be. However, sometimes we just have to realise when things are outside of our control and sit back and

---

[5] Asimov suggests the 3 laws of Robotics will be subverted for the good of humanity. However sound the logic is, remember we almost ended up with Arnold Schwarzenegger instead of Will Smith. Yep, look it up.

relax until the monitoring system alerts us that things are back.

Ultimately infrastructure provides a foundation for applications and services to work. It should meet a minimum level of uptime and performance. Anything above a minimum is a bonus. And this should be, in most cases, easy to achieve. A mail server will happily process mail endlessly. A router will route packets around your network for EVER. Uptimes of 5-10 years on networking equipment isn't even that rare[6].

It's obviously prudent to allow for growth, via performance and capacity. Good architecture is going to allow for scale out and/or scale up as needed. But let's remember that what we are ultimately doing is designing systems to mitigate risk. Big fancy racks of gear are lovely, but they need to do the work and they need to provide value back to the business. The big secondary backup system is no good if it's never utilised or it's there for a system that didn't need it in the first place.

So back to where the good news is – applications.

Applications are where IT people help businesses derive value. If you always stay in an infrastructure space, you're missing out on providing value to the business.

It can be difficult and daunting to step into this space if you've never really attempted it before.

---

[6] See Note 2

But I would strongly encourage you to start, even just looking out for small opportunities you can see to help a system or process "be better".

We do it all the time within IT. We automate SEO builds or server configurations. We write scripts or apps to make our lives easier.

So, time to start doing this for everyone else in the business.

How exactly do you do this? Like being a great therapist, you need to start listening to the people around you and finding out what their pain points are.

Some of those will be easy. The screams of frustration across the cubicles and hallways will identify problems quickly.

Others are going to be more difficult to discover. However, if you've never done this in your organisation and if you pay attention, you're going to find them pretty quickly.

I would listen to teams around reporting times, end of the month, end of the quarter etc.

There's not one company I know of that enjoys reporting periods at all. They are slow, tedious and cause tremendous amounts of pain for most organisations.

Every time I've attempted to delve into the processes, I find things that as an IT professional make me want to bang my head against a wall.

Stuff like copying reports into Excel to modify the way data is presented. Manually comparing datasets to find results, tedious manual typing of data from one system to another.

> *"Why are you using Excel as a reporting tool?"*

> *"Well because the report we get doesn't have things in the format that our Manager likes?"*

When I looked at their report, it was something the IT team (us/me) had written and had complete control over.

> *"Hey, what about if we just modify the report for you?"*

> *"You could really do that? It would save me about a day a month"*

In that moment there were tears, people started randomly applauding across the office.

Ok, there wasn't really applause[7]or any tears, but there was an enormous amount of gratitude and relief that there was a better way.

Remember, people don't know what you do...blah blah. Yeah, it's getting tiresome, but remember

---

[7] There never is. NEVER in any of those stories you've heard about people randomly clapping at airports or shops when a person gets told off. Nobody ever claps.

this means people don't know what you can do for them.

How email servers work may as well be magic to most people and they couldn't care less. Hell, I know how they work, and it bores me to tears.

Imagine, though when you can tap into the magic of a system for a user and produce a useful report that saves them time and energy. That is actually quite revolutionary for a user. But it's mundane and something that most IT people can do in their sleep.

I see a lot of complaining about the general work population using Excel as a reporting tool. I can conclude from this, two things:

1. If all you have is a hammer, everything will look like a nail
2. IT people are not helping their colleagues to get the reports they need

I can understand that Excel is actually quite useful for data manipulation. But there's a great piece of software call Microsoft SQL Server. The most under utilised system ever has to be Reporting Services in MSSQL.

However, end users usually get Excel, and nothing else. So why do we blame them when they use the tools, we give them?

One argument I hear is that giving out permissions to SQL database is scary and dangerous. Think of the damage a user could do!

Have you seen the damage users have done to workplace efficiency without the right tools?

I'm pretty sure read-only access to some database tables is the least concern for the person with their name on the building.

Time really does equal money. Paying someone $1000s a year to do some terrible Excel based data manipulation through the lack of any outside initiative for improvements is downright criminal compared to the amount of dollars the IT team might be getting paid to look down their nose and snigger at those employees.

A question I was recently asked by a young accountant was:

"Hey, can I get Python installed on my computer. I want to run some scripts to do some improved statistical analysis of our companies cashflow"

I almost fell off my chair. Well figuratively anyways.

You can bet I was first in line to give this guy Python on his PC and find out what plans he had for it. I'm no statistician, so when he explained what he was trying to accomplish and how it worked, I just nodded politely and tried to hide my ignorance of the specifics.

When I went back in a few weeks to see how he had gone, I was pleasantly surprised. He had some impressive charts, graphs and insights into the business that was reported back to the directors.

He had moved on from spending days creating reports, to spending his time discussing insights about the data with the decision makers.

This is where the value is in data. There is no value, beyond compliance reasons to be producing reports for report's sake. The value comes through gaining insights and information from your data.

Installing Python on everyone's PC is not going to make them infinitely more productive. Nor is giving everyone access to all the data stored in SQL databases in your organisation.

But if you can help show people how you can help them to leverage that data into usable information and insights into their day-to-day operations you can be far more useful to a company than adding another 9 to the uptime of their mail server.

Changing this dynamic is not easy….at all.

By creating little spots of success throughout a business, a spot of gold success shining out from a sea of grey mediocrity, it can have an enormous potential to build a wave of change throughout an organisation.

It's easy to stand up in front of people at a meeting and go through a report creator software tutorial. I suspect you will get poor attendance and no matter how amazing your presentation is I'd probably be bored by creating reports.

However, if you make the effort to find some quick wins,   a   few   places   where   some   small improvements to data can be made, you'll start to find some allies to the revolution.

Imagine sitting in meetings where users tell everyone else how amazing that new report you created for them is. You may not need to announce that it only took 10 mins and you changed the column order and the data sort.

It can take quite a while. I've spent months and months off and on with users trying to assist them, getting reports correct, data displayed in just the right format. As we slowly hone things into a polished system, they slowly realise, what took me days now takes me minutes.

Then the lightbulb goes off in their minds. Ok, now I get how this is useful.

Reporting is obviously just one aspect. But it's probably universally a great first step for any organisation.

If you're looking for areas, I'd suggest you follow your data flows. That is where you are going to find the places for improvements. Ingesting data, manipulating data and reporting data.

   "We get data in this format and we need to upload it to the system in another format."

There's plenty of tools to use to solve this problem. Don't be afraid to fire up Visual Studio or your IDE of choice and create some custom software. A day or two writing a custom app can save 1000s in manpower every day.

These are small changes though. A new report here, a change in workflow over there. But it adds up. Not just in the hours you're saving the company, but in the radical change in thinking the company is having about IT. If something isn't working well, IT can help make it better.

What you are actually trying to bring is a *digital transformation*.

This is a phrase that's often associated with companies that create APIs for everything, and ride scooters between campus buildings.

You haven't ridden a scooter since you were a kid, and you have one office, not a campus.

However, as you bring about small changes, consider the longer-term aspects of digital transformation. Small changes are one thing, but if you start a groundswell of change you want to get your surfboard ready to ride that wave.

One thing a lot of you are probably shouting at me as you read this glammed up digital transformation success story is:

> *"There is no way I have that much time in my day to do this for other people"*

And you are probably right. You are working 80 hour weeks keeping things working using string and two tin cans.

Then for those of you, I would say, yes you are right, you probably have other problems to deal with first. Biggest of which is you need to go back, review your Service Catalogue, and discuss with your governance team how your team doesn't match what your Service Catalogue demands of them.

If they don't listen because there is no governance team, the Service Catalogue is not taken seriously[8], then I would say work your 40 hours a week, let things catch on fire and ensure you document things in writing. Get your resume updated, find somewhere better to work.

If that sounds extreme, then enjoy working yourself to death. If you are working 80 hours a week to stop others from dying, then maybe take less extreme measures as part of your handover.

For the rest of you working slightly less hours, I would strongly encourage you to find some time each month[9] to consider assisting in some small improvements.

If you can do this consistently enough, and see big gains in productivity through your work, then you can start to consider where you spend your time.

Best case scenario is word starts to get around that you're helping to improve things. Your gut reaction to requests for help is to say, "No I'm too busy", but your reaction should be more along the lines of

---

[8] They haven't read it? I'm shocked! Well, not that shocked

[9] not even each week

"I can assist, but I only have a certain amount of time per month set aside for these tasks, let me schedule you in"

Hey, I'm totally willing but the schedule is weak and unyielding. IT is a harsh mistress.

You've got to a sort of mild tipping point which can either go a few ways.

Firstly, if you're the person who is actually doing the work you need to decide if you're the kind of guy that actually likes doing this work. Do you want more of it or can you give it to someone else?

If you're a manager then do you have anyone in your team that can actually do the work and do it well. Sometimes your team might not have that core skillset. You can muster up some small mods when asked, but maybe you can see that what you need is someone with a different core skill set.

Now it's time for some choose your own adventure. What are you going to do?

Are you going to outsource this project? Skip to page 112

Are you going to run this project in-house? Continue reading below …

Internal Digital Transformation

You're going to run with this digital transformation. Doing this internally is a great way to retain control and utilise the existing knowledge of the company and how it operates to improve productivity through IT improvements.

However, it's very unlikely that you have the capacity to take on more and more digital transformation.

How do we make room for it? The only way you can handle this is to get more bodies working in IT. I know lots of people are going to say there's no way anyone is going to hire more staff to cover this.

Maybe that's entirely true at first. Later down the track if you've made great improvements and real transformation you should have excellent cause to show that your transformation work is having great impact to the company and saves a ton of money. Based on that, you should be able to hire staff to cover your old work and let you continue on with what is effectively a new role.

But it's hard to get small teams to expand to an entire other team member before the results are in. Your experience may differ, but it could be tough.

If you are doing some great digital transformation work, you probably aren't a junior straight out of school. There may be enough basic stuff to push to a graduate, or a trainee or even a part time employee. You don't necessarily need to replace yourself 1:1. This may be a much easier transition for the company to make.

I'd suggest another route.

If you are starting down a digital transformation route, is there benefit from your IT team from doing all the regular stuff that IT teams do? Specifically, your internal team? Is there benefit, cost wise to outsourcing some of the more basic tasks to an MSP? You can potentially get some benefits for a percentage of the cost of a full-time employee. So rather than another $100k right off the bat for an employee, you pay $25k for an MSP to take on some of the tasks you don't want to deal with, say basic helpdesk stuff and/or server management.

While lots of teams are a bit hesitant to let others take control of the environment, it can be a big benefit for others to take on some of the more basic work, at a reasonable cost to the business, to allow you to continue to do more specialised work.

The benefit here, is that this arrangement has the potential to scale nicely, with your internal team's requirements and workload.

You can start small and offload more or less as you feel comfortable and as you need.

Think of it as flexible employee time.

Then as requests come into your team for digital transformation work you can say yes more often with the stipulation that more work is going to mean more cost for the MSP coverage. However, the benefits to the business are potentially far greater than that cost.

Not everyone is going to love this, but for smaller teams, it can be extremely useful to have an arrangement like this in place. Even for coverage under normal circumstances. Do you have team members away, need some coverage for holiday periods, company events, or extended leave?

Lots of IT teams and employees feel like an island. We have to do everything ourselves and be amazing 100% of the time at it. The reality is that trying to do that makes for unhappy employees and inflexible teams that can't cope with the flexible demands of their organisations.

The bonus of this is that it reveals the costs of this flexibility directly to everyone involved. Far too often IT teams suck it up and do the work at their own expense, of extra hours, extra stress, etc. Having an MSP to take up that extra work as needed can ensure that the business covers the costs, not the employees.

If the cost of another employee is $100k while your MSP costs are below that on a yearly basis, you have no real justification for bringing on another resource[1]. Once that changes you have the ability to then consider another internal resource, or even just continue with the MSP.

Finding an MSP that will engage in this way may be difficult but being clear at the outset of what you require is helpful to ensuring a great

---

[1] From a pure cost perspective anyways. There are other factors to consider

relationship with them. They after all are in it for the money. Doing your boring dirty work is not necessarily exciting for them from a career perspective, only from a monetary perspective. So be upfront and honest from the start.

Remember, digital transformation is the real money maker from the company's perspective, and you are the star, making it happen. Nobody cares who patches servers anyways. They didn't even realise it was you doing it 12 months ago anyways.

Outsourcing your Digital Transformation

While digital transformation is exciting and different, there are times when it's not quite in your wheelhouse of skills. You can't be an expert on everything and while you can learn most anything from YouTube these days, you don't necessarily want to.

Some areas of the business might not be your area of expertise either. While the technology is not so much the challenge the specific business area might not be a match for you.

This is not the end of the world though. Just because you identified an area for transformation doesn't mean you need to be the one with your name in the code.

In these cases, finding someone who can do the work for you can ensure that a solution is created and implemented.

Taking away the ego from the equation; does it really matter who solves the problem? Not really. The main thing is that it gets done.

Depending on what you are trying to solve, and the skills involved, the right resource could be hard to find. However, once you have a resource you can quickly scope out a project and get some costs for the work involved.

This is critical. As with hiring an MSP to cover your internal work you are able to assign a cost to the skills, work, and project that you are looking at doing.

You're able to work with the business to say, yes, we can get this work done, it will cost $X. This helps engage the business by directly exposing them to the costs associated. It might sound like a great project and super easy to them. You may have tried to tell them that what seems easy is actually massively complicated on par with building the space shuttle, but until a 3rd party actually agrees with you, they may never listen.

Internal IT teams are free right? They come with the building and cost nothing? Here's your chance to help educate them on what it costs for great IT work.

If a department is keen for transformation work, it should ultimately be up to them to take on the responsibility of providing the business case for the work. It may cost a million dollars but make back 10x that amount in 12months. They need to demonstrate that.

You should be their biggest ally in this discussion[2] and assist as you can. Otherwise, if it may just be forced back onto the internal IT team to come up with the solution as a 3rd party costs too much. It might ultimately make sense for the IT team to do the work, but it costs something, and you can't just take on a million-dollar project for nothing.

However, assuming you find the right resource and get the budget approved, the biggest piece of advice I can offer is to ensure the project is 100% scoped correctly. You pay a million dollars for work and everyone knows what you will get for that work. Down to the exact number of lines of code you require.

This is a two-way street. The business comes up with the requirements, which you need to ensure you are involved with. They go off and do the work, and the 3rd party delivers what was agreed.

It likely assumed that the 3rd party is going to try and screw you with bad code, or incomplete solution, but more times than not, it's going to be scope creep and poor planning on the business side that will make this project a mess.

Be firm. The project includes the original scope and the original deliverables. If possible, break these down into small parts and smaller

---

[2] As long as you believe it's a sound investment

deliverables, so that everyone gets a taste of how this works.

But don't let the business start adding to the scope, just a feature here or a "it would be great if we could just…".

Ultimately the IT team is delivering the work via a 3rd party. Requests come to you. If you find the business leader is calling the 3rd party guys late at night with requests, then you're probably doomed to failure.

It doesn't always need to be this strict. In the past, I've partnered with companies that have done digital transformation work that involved database upgrades and centred around business divisions I didn't really know well. We found a great partner who could do the work we needed at a good price and who worked well with our IT team.

Over time as the relationship developed and matured enough that the business unit was working directly with our partner with very little input from the IT team. The partner knew how the IT team preferred to have upgrades delivered, and what was important to us. The business unit had reasonably defined workflows that were mature enough to be easily translatable into new database formats etc.

This was great for everyone involved, in that a large volume of legacy databases were transformed, the IT team was able to guide the work as they saw fit, but the business unit took on the costs and saw the benefits. A real win-win for everyone involved.

Finding value is like discovering gold

After spending time in a gold mine I feel 100% qualified to tell anyone and everyone the intricacies of mining. It seems to me that mining for gold[3] starts off as something that is trivial and easy.

1. You find gold in specs and flakes in a creek or river.
2. Everyone with a pan and a shovel rushes to the creek and surrounding areas
3. People spend 1000s of hours sifting through the mud and discovering a reasonable amount of gold
4. After a reasonable amount of mud has been sifted no gold remains
5. Companies come in with modern mining equipment, and sift through ALL of the mud, then the rocks and down to the core of the earth
6. Company finds small amounts of gold in 1000s of tons of rocks and makes profit

---

[3] Other metals may vary

It starts as something easy. Anyone can pan for gold and in the right spot, you can find a reasonable amount of it, to make it worthwhile.

After that though, it gets harder and requires more expertise.

This is essentially how it works with finding value in IT.

At first, anyone can throw a shovel around and find areas to make improvements. However, over time it requires more expertise and skill.

What we've looked at is generally the initial phases of a digital transformation through a company. Smallish changes, quick wins, happy employees.

However, a complete digital transformation within a company requires some heavy-duty equipment, tools and skills.

Starting small is still the way to start this transformation. There is a massive cultural shift that needs to happen to make a real wave of change throughout a company.

At some point though, if you can make enough small ripples to create the start of a wave, you need to ensure you there to help drive what that looks like.

With enough momentum, this should go well beyond a simple IT team and be something of itself.

There's plenty of ways to split it, names to call it. However, you want to spin it, the key part of it is going to be guidance, if not pure leadership from the IT team.

You know your systems; you know the processes and you probably have some ideas of how things should and could be run.

When you stop considering the payroll costs of one more IT guy and start thinking teams, the IT team needs to be front and centre.

However, this is time for you to do one of two things. Either roll digital transformation as a group within IT or split and become sister teams.

What you do will depend on your company. However, if you are going down this path of full-on digital transformation, I'd give you these tips:

- IT people know "digital" and should be heavily involved
- Digital transformation requires input from the business, not just assumed that IT can fix everything. Any new resources should include non-IT people
- Digital transformation is different from everyday IT. There may be overlap but they are not the same
- Senior leadership should be heavily involved in creation, setup, and ongoing performance. If it's not discussed at a senior leadership meeting, it's not going to be successful.
- Early on you need to create a roadmap and determine what success looks like for digital transformation in your business

- Quick wins and direct impact from the team is critical to ensuring it's not a flashy money pit of an idea
- Consider seconding people into your team for short time frames to ensure you are getting a range of input, giving people ownership of the overall concept, and setting yourself up for success when you roll out new concepts and plans

If you do all these things, you are on a path to not failing. It will be incredibly difficult, but if you can pull off real transformation in your business, it can ultimately lead you to incredible company success. The companies that stagnate are doomed to be the same forever if best and most likely fail. Companies that harness innovation and transformation are on the path to being amazingly successful and dynamic, exciting place to be a part of.

Building Amazing Teams

The phrase "team building" generally sends shivers down the spines of most IT people. It conjures up images of trust falls, new corporate slogans, having to do getting to know you exercises with colleagues. I always feel slightly out of place, very pessimistic about any new corporate slogans and/or promises and keen to get back to the office to do the tasks that are far more important than team building.

One day the introverts will gain enough courage to tell the extroverts that we hate this kind of thing. We'll leave a strongly worded, anonymous letter around the office one day.

I expect that if we sent everyone who enjoyed team building days to them, they would have a great day. Meanwhile, everyone who hated them, would enjoy a quiet day in the office, while relishing the opportunity to complain about team building days and discussing in the breakroom how they are relieved not to be forced to go on the day.

However, the big realisation comes in the following days. One of the overly keen team builders exclaims how great of a day it was "We passed an egg between all of us without using our hands!"

You catch a glimpse of your "remainder" colleague giving you a look like Jim from The Office to camera. You both realise in that moment it WAS a great day for everyone.

Obviously, most IT departments discovered long ago the secret to team building was alcohol.

It may or may not be proceeded by a vendor conference where you spend the entire day hassling salespeople, deriding corporate speakers.

It may include Go Karting.

But being out of the office, having free drinks, bitching about work, and having some dinner is how IT teams are formed. I know IT departments that did this weekly. Those guys were tight[1].

So, IT teams know how to bond. The system is perfected. But how do we design our teams for maximum effect.

---

[1] I've been flown halfway around the world at eye watering expense to drink with an international IT team. It seemed extravagant at the time, but in hindsight it was 100% worth every penny. Business Class was probably a little overkill, but I'd never admit that to anyone.

It's important to determine what you actually need out of your IT team. This is in a large part going to be determined by your service catalogue.

Your service catalogue will help determine what kind of technical skills you need. This is certainly an important starting point.

It won't tell you what kind of personalities you need on your team.

Personality > Skill

Anyone with an IT career can be cross trained on a range of things. Infrastructure guys with Windows background can be Citrix guys within no time. Cisco guys can be Aruba guys. Delving into programming can be more difficult and is not a skill that comes easily to everyone. But moving from one programming language to another can be simple enough at a basic level. It's all just if/else for/next etc. You just need to learn the syntax. I'm talking basics here, not kernel development. Programmers don't have a heart attack.

Skills can just be brought in if needed. Get a consultant to handle that SAP development you don't want to tackle. It's going to cost[2] but it's all economics.

But building real teams which function effectively, communicate together, and don't end up killing

---

[2] SAP costs will make business class flights look like a cheap lunch.

each other is more than a simple combination of skill sets.

Great teams are more than the sum of their people.

The most important part of teams is to remember that IT people aren't robots. We can seem like we are robots at times, but I think a lot of IT people enjoy moderate change in their daily routines. Not too much, but given the same responsibility, the same tasks, same users, same systems most IT people will quickly burn out on them.

We tend to like to treat people like a basic function in a great arrangement when people are much more dynamic.

Staleness

As such while we tend to imagine that we bring the same level of aptitude or devotion to each incident, service request, change or problem, this is not the case. This can be a real hidden issue within IT. If Bob sees the same error message(s) every day, after a while he can get demotivated and desensitised to its meaning. That problem he once tried to solve with gusto, is now relegated to a rainy day.

It becomes stale. Bob becomes stale. He might have more enthusiasm for other parts of his role, but for this problem it's been put in the too hard basket.

This is a worry because something important might have been inadvertently hidden. You may have a ticking time bomb of a problem.

But it might not be something obvious. It may just be a glance at a system and less care given to it over time. It seems like it's working ok and therefore we move to other issues.

Everyone has a propensity to become desensitized to things over time.

So now you have potentially two problems. A system that needs attention, and an employee who is becoming unmotivated and, on the path, to being ineffective, and potentially, ultimately leaving the business.

While it's easy to try and fit teams as strictly defined links in the chain, it will be the ultimate death of your team to view things this way.

Identifying staleness and giving people some freshness is tough. You need to be proactive; you need to know your team. But not identifying the problems, letting things stew is going to give you much larger problems in the end.

What makes teams great?

It's hard to create an amazing team if you haven't defined exactly what makes a team great.

Here's a few key traits that make great teams:

- autonomy

- united in their mission
- communicate effectively with each other and their manager
- understand each other's strengths and capitalise them
- not afraid to admit mistakes
- not afraid to fail quickly
- receive clear feedback on their performance

Rather than go into each one in detail and provide some inspiring examples for each one, consider your current situation. Do your actions as a part of team or as a leader of a team help to encourage this behaviour or are they potentially detrimental to the process?

Often the things we do daily as leaders seem helpful but can be actually working against these goals.

Do we stifle people by micro-managing them? Have endless meetings to discuss progress rather than letting people actually get on with the work?

We all talk about hiring great people, but there's no point hiring people and then not trusting them to do the work you hired them to do. It sounds simple but this is something I see constantly. Whether it's by design or just by not allowing tasks to be delegated, so many managers never give up certain authority to their subordinates to allow them to get on with the job.

This happens particularly with spending money in IT. Many a time there's corporate processes for buying stationary but getting some cables or other a portable HDD or other small items are next to impossible. Why? Are you as a manager worried your team might actually buy something useful? Do you think your employees are going off to buy candy or magic beans?

These are the same employees you give Domain Admin rights to, or to maintain your firewall. Yet in other areas they have to coming begging.

I've seen plenty of people go nuts on stationary accounts, but I've seen more than my share of IT teams who couldn't get a USB cable if they tried.

If you are the one who needs to approve every purchase request, every change ticket, every single code check-in then you haven't really trusted your team.

You hired these people them, give them some trust. Allow them to do their job.

If nothing gets done when you're not in the office, if you have a queue of people at your office door the minute you get in, chances are you probably are feeling overwhelmed yourself. Think about how your team feels.

As a person I love to overthink things. I think most people stand in the shower having practice arguments for conflict that never happens. The thing with overthinking is that nobody likes it. We love to think through things and plan but staying up late at night not sleeping because of something you've down is the worst feeling in the world.

A portion[3] of this overthinking stems from my performance in the office. Are people happy with what I did yesterday? Will my manager be upset about a comment in a ticket? Am I going to be fired due to some other long outstanding issue I haven't fixed yet?

Throughout my career, I've consistently felt entirely let down as part of any review process that I've been a part of. I can't say they've all been horrible, but I can't recall one where I feel like the 30-60 mins I've spent allowed for a comprehensive debrief of my year's performance.

When I have had the opportunity to have the conversations more regularly the answer seems to generally be, "don't overthink it, everyone is happy with what you are doing".

It may be simple but having this kind of feedback is enormously helpful and confidence building as an employee going about my daily work.

Many times, managers and bosses are simply to overwhelmed, too busy, to give this type of feedback, because they are too busy dealing with the employees that they need to hear about because of all the terrible things they are doing on a daily basis.

So as a competent employee who just gets things done, it's easy to be left to your own devices.

---

[3]   Other large portions come from general emotional instability, feelings of inadequacy etc

Having this positive feedback can seem like just emotional neediness. If it is then you need help and not a hug from your boss.

However, having some constant validation of your work is important. It helps to ensure that everyone is on the "same page". Even if nothing unusual is happening, being told that you are in fact doing the right thing, in the right way at the right speed is useful feedback to get.

Having someone to help validate your choices/actions in difficult situations is absolutely critical for ensuring that you feel like you've said the right thing, taken abuse, corrected bad behaviour etc. If you see it with your direct reports or even colleagues, it's exceptionally critical to ensure that good behaviour is welcomed. You're not a dog, you don't need positive reinforcement to continue doing the right thing all day long. However, as a person you do want to feel like your hard work, especially in the face of unfounded criticism is in fact appreciated by others.

It can be especially difficult as a manager in a busy role, to be focusing on fighting fires every day. The great employees you have are doing great things every day and just the fact that you are not focusing on them, may be on your "one less thing to deal with" pile. Let those guys know that. Too often great employees are ignored or forgotten, because they don't need anyone to get them through the day. They work completely autonomously and there's nothing they need.

Maybe it seems that way, but a friendly check in and a positive word every now and again goes a long way. It helps to build confidence, let employees know you trust them. I'd rather know that I'm being ignored due to trust, than ignored due to being forgotten.

It can be easy to just let the relationship be just that.

> *"you're great, keep doing stuff, while I focus on trouble areas. Thanks for not being a trouble area"*

This may seem like a great dynamic. It can be convenient for everyone involved. However, for the non-trouble employee this can be a pathway to staleness, mediocrity, and stagnation.

Your great employee could be an even greater asset, but it's up to you to help them get there. They may not need much, but to get the maximum potential is going to need you to assist them along the path.

Great employees can turn into stagnate employees easily enough through a company's inaction. Don't waste a great employee becoming even better and doing more for your organisation. Chances are your great employees are going to get better even without your help. If there's no path, no care and nowhere for them to grow in your organisation, then there's lots of other companies out there looking for a new great employee.

This is a big reason people will move to another job. They are overlooked and feel the need to look elsewhere for opportunities.

In that last yearly review you discussed how their salary is indexed to a state average for their job[4]. It was hard work on your part to get that 2% raise for them. What I hear in those conversations is how the company has worked out how much they can pay me without me looking for another role.

For a lot of people this is going be reassuring news. Boy am I glad I'm not looking for a role right now, the job market is tight. Change definitely seems too hard.

For IT people this is going be viewed as a challenge.

> *"The company doesn't think I can beat the average. I'll show them!"*

Most of the time they are right.

Sometimes you just aren't going to have the right roles, growth, and capacity to keep that great employee around as they grow. This is perfectly fine and reasonable. Moving on is not necessarily an admission of failure by both parties. However, I can't remember the last time I saw a perfectly amicable split between employee and company.

I've seen rival IT companies with offices on each side of the street, trade employees almost weekly.

---

[4] Yes, this happened to me. Yes, it pissed me off.

Employee in Company A has nowhere to go in the company, finds job in Company B and gets the promotion and pay rise they were looking for. 18 months later the same employee goes back to Company A for the next promotion they were after.

Trading employees like sports teams. But it was to the benefit of the employees and not the company.

Huge recruitment costs, massive amounts of work to hire and rehire the same people. For the amount commissions I hear these recruitment companies take as a fee, you would think that either company or both would start to think about how to promote from within. Yet nothing ever changed.

It doesn't have to be this way. IT leaders have been in this position over and over again. We can help to break these cycles.

Hiring Great People

Everyone wants to hire the *"best"* people. Lots of companies think that they **only** hire the best people. Unless you're owned by a slightly eccentric billionaire, then you are definitely not at a company that hires only the best people.

That's ok. What defines a person as the best is:

- a matter of opinion
- depends on the team that surrounds them
- heavily influenced on the willingness of the person to apply themselves
- nurture from great managers and teammates
- determined by the challenges given to them in their role
- usually not determined solely by which school they went to

To be honest, most of the time you actually don't need the very *best* person anyways. What you want is a great individual who helps make them team better. You want someone who you, as a manager, or colleague or company can hire and help build to be better when they finished than when they started.

Job hunting and hiring people is generally terrible. For those applying for jobs it feels like nothing is ever a perfect fit, job requirements are crazy and writing custom resumes for each job you apply for seems weird and difficult. Cover letters seem like a half page begging session for a role you don't even know you want.

"Why do you want this role?"

"Um, so I have money to buy food and maybe some cool stuff."

On the other side, it's difficult to weed out the wheat from the chaff. People can be desperate for a job and so apply for anything, anywhere. Others undersell themselves and can be discounted too early. Some people are terrible at interviewing. How can you really get to know someone in a 30 min interview?

It helps to break things down into some core questions to ask ourselves about candidates.

Questions to ask yourself of a potential employee:

- Can they do the job? There's a basic requirement to be actually qualified and capable.
- Would they fit into the team? Are they the same as the rest of the nerds? Is that what

you are looking for? Could they complement you team in ways you might not expect?
- What else do they bring to the company
- Could they be valuable in a different role?
- Can you help them grow?

This is purely a starting place for evaluating candidates.

I've seen some places that try and evaluate candidates on a single 30 min interview. Others have a lengthier process.

What works best for you is going to be determined largely by the company, the role, and the candidate to you are interviewing. Just like writing a custom resume or cover letter for each role you apply for, it's perfectly acceptable in my opinion to tailor your hiring process to each individual as well.

Obviously, you are trying to eliminate candidates at each phase of your process, whether that's early on at a resume phase, or introductory phone call, or interview.

However, it's important to remember that candidates hopefully are good at their job, but they may not be great in the selection process.

It's all too easy to eliminate candidates for things that ultimately aren't important for the job we are hiring them for.

Lots of IT people are not great in interviews.

- Should a single interview preclude them from the process?

- Should our process for candidates be more than just a few short interactions?
- Is resume filtering software the best thing since actually having to read resumes?

Well, obviously I do otherwise I wouldn't have asked rhetorical questions like that.

I hate writing resumes and I dislike non-technical people reading them. I've sat in countless interviews where the interviewer has a list of job requirements and then goes through my resume to find where I've included the requirements. Sometimes in complete silence without even asking me anything about each of the requirements. Needless to say, we didn't really click.

A role needs to have a definition of what is involved and some thought to experience that makes a candidate qualified for that role.

But IT roles can be deceptive and experience on a resume can be just as deceptive. Again, this is a great scenario where we try and pigeonhole people into categories for the ease of decision making. This can lead to horrible decisions around whether a candidate has enough experience or skills to do a certain role.

I know people whose resume vastly under-describe the things they did in certain roles. IT Manager in one company means a completely different thing in another. Trying to describe that in a few paragraphs is far too difficult.

Trying to line up a resume line by line to a job description is dumb way to evaluate people. Just like putting a wish list of requirements is a great way to end up with an overly qualified employee for an entry level role. If it's designed for a graduate don't expect them to have experience.

The more senior a role you are trying to hire for, the more you are going to need to look beyond the resume. No two careers are the same and one with a few more curves along the way may lead to a great candidate.

Once you get past resumes and you are looking to engage further with candidates then look to go beyond a simple asking of "what do you know about the company".

There is no point in being a strict schoolmaster in an interview when you're a much more laid back as a manager. You can laugh, have fun, and generally enjoy talking with people. I think employers forget that the evaluation is happening on both sides of the table.

You should be the same in the interview room as you are outside of it. How you are inside of it also should reflect the nature of the company itself.

Interviews are an extended negotiation for each side. It should start off as an employee relationship should and be a relatively friendly one. The candidate is someone you are potentially going to have to trust, and rely on, so treat it accordingly.

Formal interviews can be quite intimidating to some candidates and they don't perform well in these circumstances. This might be especially true of your standard introverted IT professional. Having some compassion and understanding in these circumstances can go a long way.

Having candidates performing programming tasks, or infrastructure processes short or long is a great way to change up the standard 30 min back and forth. This is a fantastic way to evaluate a technical portion of a candidates resume. Programming challenges are not unusual, but for infrastructure, sysadmin types it's not the most common. I love to do this as soon as I see a candidate in front of a server, I can quickly gauge their ability through their confidence using an interface, running commands and how they problem solve.

I've used this technique quite a few times with candidates and it's a great technique.

Giving candidates something new and watching how they solve a problem or scenario is an excellent way to evaluate them. The end result is not the most important as much as the process they took to get there.

So, putting them in front of a type of firewall they have never used before and asking them to perform certain tasks is a great way to find out who knows the concepts and who passed the certification by rote.

Another unusual but effective method is to get a potential candidate in front of the rest of the team.

In previous roles it became standard that the entire team of 8-10 people had breakfast with the candidate at a restaurant. The whole process was completely informal. It didn't give all of the team an opportunity to chat in depth with a candidate, but it did give everyone a chance to get a sense of them. For those 3-4 who spent more time interacting it gave them a great sense of their character and personality.

In that company the team then was given veto power on the candidate. If anyone had a strong objection, they could raise it and the candidate would be rejected.

This was a great way to evaluate the candidate interacting with the team in a very informal social way. It also was extremely powerful in giving the team power in the process and say if they ever thought someone wrong was going to be hired.

In my time there I don't think anyone ever rejected a candidate at that stage but having the ability and transparency through the process was certainly a great sign of confidence from management to the team.

While having an hour or so to chat with the team as a candidate is a great way to gauge future interaction.

Is it perfect? No. But it's more than a 30 min interview[1].

Ultimately until they start you can never fully get an idea of how they fit into a workplace.

It is critical that in the beginning you have set clear expectations and given your new employee every opportunity for success. However, if things are not working out, you need to ensure you are putting things in place to correct anything you need to, or ultimately if that doesn't work, letting the employee go.

If you have a system of an initial probationary period of employment, it's critically important you use that time to ensure you get to the end of it 100% committed to having your new employee in the team forever.

If not then depending on the employment law in your area, you can terminate the employee in the first 3, 6 or 12 months as part of their probationary period without a long, drawn-out process.

It might seem harsh to be talking this way, however, you want to have people on your team that fit in and perform well. There are lots of reasons why people don't succeed in a role, but if your new employee isn't the super star you wanted, or their personality doesn't fit the team,

---

[1] Sometimes a 5 min interview is more than enough to know

it's time to correct their behaviour early and/or find someone else.

Having one bad employee is the best way to drag down an entire team of great employees.

I'd rather ensure my existing team is happy than my one new guy.

However, don't let the potential for disappointment discourage you from the excitement of bringing in new and different people into your team. I think a little conflict and passionate exchange of different ideas from different people in a team is a great method for success.

Don't be afraid to look outside the norm for employees that have the potential to bring a different perspective, or experience to your team.

It can be difficult to hire someone for a graduate role that's in their 50s. But at the same time if you are looking for a great programmer, why discount someone who is a little older with only a few years on the language you need. Dig deeper and you may find that they have a wealth of programming experience, not only on the language you need, but also on programming languages that went extinct before you were even born.

I don't want the takeaway to be *diversity for diversity's sake*. But don't discount people for any reason. IT is certainly a heavily male dominated industry, but that's definitely to our detriment as a whole. IT ladies are as perfectly capable as the men. Unlike everywhere else, where I've made sweeping generalisations, I'll be slightly more careful and say that the ladies I've worked with in IT are fantastic. Some are highly technical; some are great problem solvers; all of them competent in their roles and brilliant to work with. What they have to deal with the industry as women is complete BS and the fact that they even persist in it is something we should be extremely grateful for.

I would be a complete idiot[2] to discount someone "because they are a woman" or a different ethnicity, or race, or education or social class. None of those things have ever made a difference about whether someone was competent in their role.

Just don't discount anyone, and don't discount having some differences in personality in your teams. Variety is the spice of life as they say. The best teams aren't made up of one person copied 7 times over. You can't just have opposites in a room working until they kill each other one by one until a winner is determined by who survives either. The best teams are a complex interconnect of different people supporting, arguing, competing, challenging each other. Anything else is just robots working in silence.

---

[2] Other verbs may apply also

A Real World Example

"I work for a company with 8 different branches. I recently took over the job as sysadmin/I.T. manager. I have found out quick that we are the last to know about anything affecting us. Today my team called me letting me know the HQ superintendent decided to shut down the power in thirty minutes to the entire building. Apparently, they had this scheduled for weeks.

I called the super and asked what was going on. "Yeah well last time we got yelled at for not letting you guys know so now we let you know 30 mins in advance." Why. Just why. My major hardware components are all on UPS backups. Everything ended up fine besides a few small hiccups....but what if it didn't. What if I hadn't cleaned up that network closet when I started 5 months ago. What if I didn't get to cleaning up that mess yet and installing battery backups? All 7 other branches would have had no connection to HQ servers. This is my first sysadmin job. Are we always the last to know or is this just a company flaw? Am I upset for no reason?"

Ok so this is a real rant[1] on reddit. The frustration is obvious. We have a guy in his first sysadmin role guy trying his best to do the right thing, not being told things that are important to the continued running of the company.

There are some great things happening with this guy. First sysadmin role, but he's taken some initiative to clean up server rack, install a UPS. He's come into the role, considered the state of affairs, and made some great improvements to the infrastructure. Well done.

Now he's finding himself out of the loop on information he needs.

I feel like this is a classic situation a lot of sysadmins face. They've done great work at the technology layer. They feel the weight of responsibility for ensuring the company is running well. He's even got some great EQ in reviewing events and looking for improvements. He knows there's an issue and wants to fix it, but unsure of the solution.

However, things breakdown outside of the network rack. There's a communication issue.

Without knowing more about the company it's hard to lay blame in any one specific reason, but I'm going to identify a few ways forward here.

---

[1] As labelled on reddit but agreed by me.

This is purely a communication issue, but it stems from an authority/respect issue.

Most likely this guy has authority over technology generally. He's clearly able to get some improvements done, with most likely some purchasing of equipment like a new UPS and some ethernet cables for a server room tidy up.

While this guy has authority over technology, he has no authority over anyone else in the company. He likely has limited respect within the company and therefore nobody is feeling like they need to communicate or ask permission for things.

This is not uncommon, by any means. Remember our rule, "*nobody knows, and nobody cares*".

This guy needs to make people care a little more. He doesn't need to start having the admiration of *<insert local sports hero>*, but he needs to have people aware enough that he starts to get in the loop.

The first step here is to ensure he reaches out to the HQ super and try and get him into a position where he communicates directly in the future. One call to rant isn't going to really help. It's just more yelling and from our Supers position, nothing has changed. Just someone else yelling.

But our sysadmin can use this incident as a way to build a relationship. He can use this to provide a way to improve the HQ Super's day. Last time he got yelled at, now he has someone to talk to that will appreciate the information, actually use it to communicate, plan and be proactive.

Now from a "boots on the ground" operational perspective there's a channel for communication that is beneficial to both parties. This is the most important part of this conversation to remember. It's providing a mutually beneficial setup.

The second step is to have a communication upwards around this issue. Now what was posted is a pretty good write up. It states the problem, potential issue, the proactive work that was done which mitigated this issue. These last steps are important to keep reminding people. It's no good avoiding an incident without reminding people of the proactive work that got you to avoiding it in the first place. You don't have to give out medals for it, but a friendly reminder upwards is important. It is also a great opportunity to give a shout out to your team to upper management as well. If Jim spotted a problem, helped to resolve it and now it saves an outage, give Jim some credit. It may sound simple and a little redundant, I mean, everyone in your team knows Jim is a great employee.

But what about more senior people in your organisation? Do they actually know what Jim does or the quality of his work? When they sign off on next year's IT budget, they may feel a lot easier paying for the $75,000 a year Jim makes when they remember he saved the organisation that much just by one great initiative.

Everyone loves to hear a success story. Especially if it's for the business they own. Even if it's simply so at the next round of golf when your CEO hears his CEO buddy complain about a power outage or bad IT, he can say "oh my IT guys fixed that last year.".

Hopefully managing up is not a big problem, as you already have a regular one-on-one with your boss, and a regular governance meeting.

Lots of IT guys would get these steps out of order. They immediately go and run to their boss and complain about the lack of information, being out of the loop, the continual way IT is treated like garbage.

However, you're a big boy (or girl) now and you have to start trying to fix the non-tech problems by yourself. Because nobody likes being dumped with a problem on their desk. Plus, you are not that guy or girl. You're a problem solver.

"Hey boss, we almost had a big issue, Jim did stuff to cover it so we didn't, and I spoke to the HQ super who will work with me in future, so communication is clear."

As a boss, that's the kind of problem I like to see. One that has already been solved.

So, everything is wrapped up nicely then. Well, this is a best-case scenario. The Super could be difficult, a massive jerk and despite your best efforts he's not on your Christmas card list.

If you're a little lowly in your company, a phone call from the sysadmin or even the IT manager, however, initially friendly, and helpful it is, may not been enough to persuade the Super to reciprocate your goodwill.

That's when your boss needs to earn his pay check as well. Nothing is as persuasive as a call from someone who pays the lease. But this should never be your first point of call.

Remember, your phone on your desk is most often the simplest, quickest, cheapest, easiest way of getting things done. Words are the sharpest and most effective of weapons.

Enterprise thinking

You've been playing games, building computers, configuring Wi-Fi and doing some programming through your teenage years. Now it's time for a real-world job. You'll most likely fall in to one of two different areas. Very large enterprise or small business.

Is a large enterprise one better than a small business?

That's a difficult question.

To quote the Simpsons, Short answer yes, with an "if". Long answer no, with a "but".

Here's the long answer.

Getting a job in a larger company, let's say something over 1000 people can be a great entry way into the full-time job market. You're not going to be the CEO, unless your dad owns a group of companies. You're going to be the lowest of the low. But that's ok. If you are starting in an entry level IT role, it's most likely a first level helpdesk job, or something where you wear a headset all day.

You'll be a small cog in a big system of gears, pulleys, and the occasional lever. The pay will be average, the job will be repetitive and after a while you can do it without thinking too hard. This is fine.

At least you will be in air-conditioning, be quiet enough to not give you permanent hearing loss, or the black lung and you won't be lifting heavy things all day. Essentially the key reasons why people like office jobs.

You will quite likely be exposed to soul crushing boredom, working for horrible bosses that ruin your day and don't know your name, annoying colleagues, and a never-ending stream of calls/tickets/work.

On the bright side there is free coffee and a ping pong table that nobody ever dares to use and a Christmas party that your social club membership kind of paid for.

The real reason you want to be there is because big companies are great to learn from. Here's my list of things you want to learn:

Procedures

Big companies have procedures, workflow, and policies. They probably suck but they exist. Most likely they are all taken from books, expert consultants, or pricey efficiency experts, implemented then poorly maintained.

This is your opportunity to get up close and personal with bureaucracy. It's a lumbering giant, with a big heart. It can't change often unless given a push from someone who's last name is on the building, and it guides everyone into knowing what the right thing to do is at every step of the way.

How to dress, where to park, how to send outbound packages, apply for leave. It's all there in company policies.

Its online systems are no doubt managed by a middle-aged lady who curates them within an inch of their life, and guards them as if they were her children (photos of which adorn her office). What she actually does day to day is questionable, but she is the keeper of the rules.

Policies and procedures exist for a number of probably reasonable reasons. For the purposes of this book, we will deal with the ones we actually care about.

Compliance and Certification

The rules exist to enable companies to get certified by companies that provide certification. Then other companies will deal with your company based on that certification. EG ISO 9001, 27001 and any other combination of numbers. Do you have a procedure around data retention, asset disposal, password changes? You probably have them to meet an ISO certification or

ISO certification is a way for a company to level up and have a more impressive LinkedIn profile. Or at least have some sense that it's not getting $400m a year in a government contract while being run out of a WeWork office.

They also exist so that when someone steals $400m from a company, legally there is a policy to point to that says you shouldn't do that. Or that someone checks to ensure someone isn't doing it.

The policy equivalent of putting a "this may contain traces of peanuts" warning on a packet of salted peanuts.

Whether certification and compliance are stupid or redundant is something not worth really discussing. At some point in your career, you will be in a position where you are thrust into discussions around compliance and certification and therefore need experience working with them and understanding what's expected.

So, while they can at times look a little redundant, understanding the reason they exist is important. And the real reason they exist is not because people think 12-character minimum length passwords are secure, it's because at one point ISO 27001 said it was secure enough.

Understanding that is the key between intelligence and wisdom.

Or at least knowing that while your system has 14 character minimum and multi factor authentication, when asked you can say that your password policy currently exceeds Sarbanes-Oxley requirements.

Are we providing tech policy just for the sake of compliance? No, not at all! Well ok sometimes we might. But at a minimum there is a basic level of IT best practise that legislatures are trying to document. Understanding what the certification and compliance landscape looks like, even at a high level, helps to take you from IT call centre jockey to something that's…. well not that.

At some point running an IT department of any size larger than 0, you will be asked about password policy. It's better to have one from an existing baseline policy you may have encountered in previous roles. Even if from a day-to-day perspective it doesn't actually do much for you.

The guy asking you about multifactor authentication is going to be super happy when you can point him to the documents that show him your ISO 27001, SOX compliance status. Especially when he has no idea what multifactor authentication is.

While it's in no way interesting to the average IT professional, being exposed early and beginning to understand this whole landscape is going to help you enormously in the future. Taking extremely close note of that those policies and procedures for future reference may also help enormously…...if you catch my drift.

Working within enterprise IT frameworks

Let's say your first job out of school is working on a helpdesk for an organisation of 5000 people. Maybe you have a helpdesk of 10 people that you all work around an open planned area with a couple of supervisors.

Most of the day your reset passwords, create new users, and fix basic problems that you have specific knowledge base articles for. Anything else gets escalated to other teams.

Well after 1 month of this role, I'd say you would have a pretty good working knowledge of how large IT teams work and a good knowledge of an IT framework most likely ITIL.

After a year you may have had some level of actual ITIL training. You've seen how it's great and how your organisation royally misunderstood it and hasn't implemented it correctly.

Password resets are annoying, but you have some grasp of how IT works in an enterprise sense.

While there are no real secrets behind a framework like ITIL, or how teams are structured, there is enormous benefits in working within an existing structure.

The initial learning curve of working within a framework, a ticketing system, phone system, corporate IT personal structure gives you the getting up to speed knowledge. You realise quickly that understanding how to build gaming computers gives you pretty much zero experience for working on a helpdesk in a procedural sense. The gaming PC stuff helps more at a desktop support level.

Enterprise IT at this phase of your career ie, step 1, is all about exposure. Seeing how large enterprises run IT departments, how they staff them, how they implement policies and frameworks.

This is really important for you early on to get a sense of what people mean when they say "Enterprise IT". There's a difference between something building gaming PCs at home, or learning some basic coding, setting up a server or two and doing it within a large organisation. And building PCs or coding or installing servers or Arduinos or anything is a great place to start, tinkering, learning etc. They are brilliant. But it's a building block (and hobby) for the next step.

Being in a large organisation can give you a great sense of not only processes and functions, but also how infrastructure is setup. How are things architected, what kind of servers, switches and storage are used? How much bandwidth do you need for an office of 500 people?

While you know the basics of IPs, routing, WiFi and home internet, what does it take to make an organisation function? What servers do they use? What type of virtualisation platform do they use?

What servers aren't virtualised? How much is in the cloud?

There's little doubt you aren't getting given full admin rights in the first 10 mins being there. But even without knowing it you are going to get an idea of what it takes from a hardware and software perspective to make people productive.

Enterprise IT can be great…..IF….you have colleagues to help you learn and nurture your growth.

If you're just another warm body on the phone to answer angry calls from users, then you're going to have to learn what you can, and look to level up into another role.

If you do have even one person to give you some extra guidance and knowledge, then learn everything you can about everything. Whether it's hardware, software, management, process etc. Especially their opinion of the state of things. Generally, you are going to make your mind up after a while about most aspects of the job, the company and IT. It's human nature to pick the bad things and have a complain after a long day. It's great practise to be fair in assessments of different things, finding the good as well as the bad. It's going to be invaluable to pick the brains of someone older and more experienced to see what they think.

Does their assessment agree with yours? What would they do differently? What things are done really well? These are great questions to always be asking yourself and colleagues you trust. If you find your initial critiques are not the same then it can be extremely useful to learning why you got the wrong impression. Was there some aspect you overlooked? Is your colleague just plain wrong? That could happen too.

Working with people

Going through school can be a tough time. You are lumped into classes of your peers, with little regard to your preference. Whether you get along with your classmates or not is of little concern to educators, except in extreme circumstances, and you are forced to deal with these people 5 days a week 40 something weeks of the year.

In the corporate world, you have some choice of employment, and high expectation of working with like-minded experienced professionals. But after a week on the help desk, you've realised your mistake. You are naught but an ear to be filled with complaint, fury, and disappointment in systems outside your control. You are the emotional release for a co-worker after a day of utter frustration. Very quickly you may start to realise you haven't started an IT job, you've started a role as emotional support for a company of emotional babies.

While this can be a source of enormous frustration, it is inevitably going to be something you need to learn how to deal with. Being in a larger company can help to accelerate your exposure to all types of working professionals and in turn help to develop those people skills.

This might be tough, or it could come easily for you. Most likely, you could be in a position where you find working with some people far easier than others. Either way you're going to be thrown in the deep end.

This probably sounds quite daunting. However, I would encourage you to view it as an enormous opportunity to start working on those people skills. Can you be known around the office as one of the "approachable" IT guys?

Simply having the broad number of different people around you every day allows you to get better and working with them and gauging your ability to do so.

What about small companies?

Working in enterprise seems to be best then? Well not necessarily. Large companies give you broad scope of experience, but at a very high level. Small companies can give you a narrower scope of experience but at a much higher level of involvement.

What is just a single team in a large company can easily be the entire company. This makes you a much larger part of the overall picture, and likely to be either:

a) a generalist, doing work in a lot of different areas in a very active sense, or

b) a specialist in one specific field, but delving much deeper into that field

There's a higher chance of you walking out the door after 2 years with a much broader or higher skill level for specific technologies, than you potentially are going to find at a larger company.

Hopefully as part of a smaller company you get a chance to work with a team that mentors and trains you. Generally, looks after you as you start in your career.

Each opportunity is going to be different than the next so it's impossible to suggest what is best. However, taking a practical and pragmatic approach to a role, understanding what you can learn, just by sitting in the building is important. The days you find things frustrating beyond measure, may be the ones you can learn from as you go into your next role. They may just be setting an important foundation to help you in the future. Especially in the days you least expect it.

IT is more than just technology

The major reason I never wavered in having a career in IT was that I enjoyed working with computers. Loved them, understood them, so a job with more computers, bigger ones, in server rooms and offices and data centres would clearly be even better. Plus, they pay you to do it! This is going to be way better than being at school. Oh, how wrong I was.

There is an excellent discussion by a UK doctor on why lots of aspects of medical training are not suited for medical students.

A lot of very smart people are trained at university and medical schools and their very smart brains filled with copious amounts of medical knowledge. These very bright people are then released into hospitals armed with their enormous medical knowledge.

On the face of it this sounds like an excellent system. Humans are anatomically extremely complicated systems that require an extreme amount of training to understand and therefore treat effectively.

The reality is that being a doctor is more about dealing with people than it is fighting disease. While they roleplay delivering bad news to patients etc at medical school. The reality is in unsurprisingly far more difficult. Coupled with the emotional difficulty that is being able to have that very real conversation with a patient, having to then move on with the rest of the day and decouple yourself is not easy.

While end of life conversations are not necessarily a common thing for a doctor to have to deal with, people are constant. Whether they are patients, family, staff etc, they are a constant that doctors have to deal with. The only test we put students through in getting to be doctors are tests of knowledge.

Hence, we get very smart people becoming doctors who may or not be good at dealing with people. As such many doctors find that the career they have chosen is not particularly suited for them. Conversely being more upfront about this requirement early and reducing academic requirements for candidates who are more balanced with an aptitude for social skills may in fact lead to better doctors. Or so is said by our UK doctor.

So as a young IT professional I was all about learning technology. This was fine for my first role in a AS/400 software company. AS/400s are an IBM produced mini mainframe of a computer that aren't something that people have at home. On the job training is required.

However, my next role was as a call centre rep for an ISP. While I didn't realise it at the time, I was in fact having to use far more skill in actually dealing with people than I did with technology.

It's taken an embarrassingly long time for me to discover the exact same thing doctors at some point discover, it's all about people.

This can be said then that working in IT is not about the technology as much as it is working with people. This can be said of lots of technical jobs, but it still comes as a shock to many. A lot of people will remain in denial of this fact and continue as if this isn't the case.

Ultimately this is to their detriment.

It may be a challenge but improving your ability to deal with the non-technical aspects of IT, dealing with people is an important skill to build.

However, depending on your own personality and/or situation you may find this too much of a challenge. The best thing to do is to at least be aware of this choice you've made.

If you really just want to be a head down, full on technical guy, then that's fine, but be aware that you are making a choice. In doing so you will need to have ways of being able to support that choice you make. By ensuring you utilise people around you well, having a manager that can support you well. It should be a factor in how you evaluate roles, and opportunities that come up.

I'm not advocating for everyone to suddenly be a larger-than-life extrovert. Far from it. There is value in understanding that most work involves people to varying degrees. Embrace that concept and find your own level of comfortableness in dealing with people.

Humanity in IT

There are strategies and plans and technologies that help make up a large part of why an IT team or company is successful.

However, the key reason a group will be successful or not is its people. And people are the hardest thing to get right.

We are as individuals, complex and in large part unpredictable. But we are also very predictable in all the ways that conflict with how corporations would like us to be.

Why do projects fail? People.

Why do start-ups fail? People.

Why doesn't your item sell on your Shopify store? People.

People are the best and the worst. I believe most of the problem when we deal with people in an IT space, we imagine in some ways that they will behave exactly like the servers and technology we also manage.

We do it through an unending pursuit of efficiency and increased productivity. At worst we treat people like the very technology they control, and at best we strive too always be better.

Let me delve into projects more. IT projects are notoriously bad at not being on time. This isn't a new problem though. IT isn't something we invented yesterday. If we are always on a course to improve things, why hasn't our IT project planning improved?

I believe we have yet to face the reality of how productive the individuals in our team actually are. We oversimplify how productive an individual can be at any one point in time. Most people when planning use some kind of constant metric for productivity when in reality our productivity levels differ widely based on 1000 different factors.

I suspect this is true of all industries but factors around each different role and job type influence how much "productivity" if we can actually measure it, fluctuates on a minute by minute, hour by hour basis.

People can be unproductive for a variety of reasons. On leave and off sick generally are the major ones we encounter, but this is generally predictable. Employees get x days of sick leave and annual leave per year. Sickness rates jump in cooler months due to colds and flu etc, by a factor of Y (you can look it up for yourself). So 2X + Y /

Z or some formula more than a random one I just made up, gives a generally acceptable rate of attendance to the office for a team. The larger the team and longer the project the more these statistics will become true. For smaller teams statistics will be meaningless, but the control over annual leave will be potentially higher.

However, these predictable rates of unattendance I don't think are the problem. We generally assume that bums on seats it a job equals a known level of performance.

This is not the case!

Everyone will have a difference level of performance, even within the same job description. From a job performance perspective, there's certainly issues with an employee who does half the work of another. Assuming a unit of is measurable and appropriate. However, let's get to job performance a little later.

Just because someone is sitting in their chair on a workday does not automatically make them 100% productive.

Before we delve too much into why that is, I think it's important to understand some context for IT roles vs other job roles and why I think that performance is and isn't (depending on the role) fluctuating more or less in any one point in time.

Job roles that are more defined and rely more on mechanical assistance in a role, can help to minimise this fluctuation. Let's talk about mining because I worked in one for some time and understand a small portion of it. Plus, it's radically different from what I suspect you are thinking about when I talk about a job.

In a mine you are digging up rocks and dirt that you hope has some mineral in it and transporting it to be refined. Generally, to transport it you get the biggest truck the mine can accommodate, load lots of rocks and dirt into the truck and that truck transports the load to a point to be refined. Some might say that's an oversimplification, but lots of mining and heavy industry work is just that simple. We dug it out of the ground then we moved it to somewhere else. Knowing where to dig in the first place is, however, more than half of the difficult part.

So, I'm in a big truck, with 50-500 tons of rock in the back of it. I spend my 12-hour shift driving this truck up and back from the same 2 points at a very slow speed. I sit stationary in my truck for large portions of the day. Stopping for lunch and rest breaks as well as filling up with fuel at a few points.

As long as I, as an employee are in some fit state for work ie able to physically get out of bed, not drunk or under the influence of drugs and reasonably well rested, I can do this job. Let's be clear, driving big machines like this is not crazy difficult. Once you learn the basics, there's a lot of monotony from in this job. It is not overly physically taxing. The cab is airconditioned so driving it in difficult external conditions, which is pretty much most mines, it isn't uncomfortable 95% of the day. It's bumpy as hell, so don't have a headache. But going between picking up rocks and dumping rocks is pretty basic from a mental stress point of view. There isn't much mental fatigue going on, only staving off boredom.

Let's be very clear, I'm not trying to disparage truck drivers in mines. But I know a bunch of them and they themselves tell me, it's boring as hell. This is true of lots of jobs. They can repetitive and monotonous. They are still important jobs to be done and I won't suggest otherwise.

For the purposes of this discussion, however, our truck over a 12-hour period may only get 10 loads completed. The laws of physics would dictate that there is a maximum number of loads that could ever be completed in a 12-hour shift which is 10. Very few things would detrimentally affect this productivity, machine breakdowns being the main one. Less factors would be the driver themselves. Someone having a bad day is still going to deliver 10 loads of rock in a day vs someone who is whistling pleasantly all day.

This can be the case for a large number of jobs. In this case the truck itself provides a fair amount of the workload and the driver a much smaller part. Their influence over the truck is therefore greatly reduced.

Even if I as the driver come down sick for the day, it would be easy to replace me with another driver and get the same 10 loads of rocks delivered for processing. Thus with 10 trucks, 2 shifts a day, a maximum 10 loads per shift. Over a 5-day work week we could assume a maximum of 1000 loads of rocks be completed. We may find that we get a 90% or greater percentage of completion for that work. At worst 900. Depending on the financial tolerance of the mine that could very well be an excellent work rate and at the very least a plan that is reliably predictable. If 1000 was the minimum they needed an investment in another truck may be all that's needed to gain that minimum. Big trucks are not cheap, but neither are mining operations. However, we have some predictability in attaining our metric, due to primarily the nature of the role.

Let's take another IT related example. I'm a programmer, which I am. I'm on a very small team of 2, to develop a killer app. How do we know when to go to market with our app?

Well first off, we need the app specs. For the sake of argument, let's say we know exactly what the app should look like and how it should function.

Ok, so owners want to know, when do we launch. There's a marketing team of 20 ready to go on this. 2 vs 20, yep I'm keeping examples real today.

Well, we break down the work. Who is going to do what? That will depend on my experience as a programmer. Have I written an app like this? What are the potential trouble spots in development? Do I have code I can reuse? What are we likely to get stuck with? Do we have a reliance on other teams such as infrastructure? Are we sure of the colours?

There's a lot to potentially break down here. But let's say we can develop a reasonably accurate work plan, there are no machines here to help do the work for us. There are only 2 programmers doing everything.

Therein lies the difference.

The first week I might come in guns blazing. I'm writing code, I'm feeling great. But I come week 3 and 4 I might come to a problem. I'm stuck in my code. It won't compile, it won't debug and not even stackoverflow can help. All I find is a thread where someone else has the same problem as me and there are no replies. Ships stuck in the doldrums of programming with not even a radio between us to mutually commiserate.

The pressure is mounting. How far behind are we? When will we ship? It might be impossible to say.

"How long is a piece of string?"

"You're being unhelpful"

"These endless meetings are unhelpful"

"Don't go home until it's fixed!"

Can you bring others to help troubleshoot your code? At this stage it would take a week to get someone up to speed. Do you work well under pressure?

Right now, the solution could be as simple as a single line of code, or even a stray character. It could require a complete redesign. Or a complete redesign could put you back in the same point.

Maybe the problem is not even in the code. Maybe the infrastructure team made a mistake, and nobody knows. Programmers don't understand the infrastructure and the infrastructure team doesn't understand code.

How do you plan for this? How do you plan to get out of this?

There isn't a single answer of course. But it shows some of the complexity of these types of roles. This is only just one (albeit fairly common issue).

Other problems you face could be more directed at individuals. Someone isn't off sick today, but all week they've felt unwell. The more they push to come into the office the worse they've felt. They can't reliably code as fast or as well as usual. More mistakes are made and by Friday they go home early after lunch as they just can't finish the day. Did we record that in our project planning models? Did we expect that programmer one makes programmer two sick and we lose more time the following week?

Does the weekend actually offer time to recuperate for programmer 1 and mentally recharge for the week, or does it only offer up a portion of what's truly needed.

Do you come into the office just feeling like being you're not productive today? Maybe you're burnt out, or just tired, or distracted or just meh. You can't just get in the truck and drive at 5 kph all day. YOU need to be the productivity and when you can't muster it, the productivity evaporates.

How and when it comes back is sometimes impossible to tell. But try explaining that to the project manager or your boss.

Some jobs are as much art as science or process. Designing creatives isn't process its art. Being a great sales guy is part process, part understanding psychology and 3 parts bullshit. It's more like performing great music.

Art by definition has no purpose other than itself. But many times, what we create is in every way art. And art is about inspiration as much or more than the perspiration that goes into creating it.

From a corporate perspective I think we don't appreciate that. Certainly, from an IT perspective I don't think we ever been able to widely acknowledge or appreciate or get respect for that. IT is just magic from an outside perspective.

Look at the Saturn V rocket. We acknowledge the science that built it, but we stand and marvel at it. If it was purely a scientific feat, why do we feel so much emotion to it?

Why, do we call a car beautiful and be amazed at an airplane. The space shuttle is described as a flying bus to space. It was over-designed to hell by a million committees, built for purposes it never actually achieved. Was way over budget, under performed as a reusable spaceship, blew up twice, and yet it every single one is preserved and admired.

Machines can be art. Software is art. Architecture is art. Whether a building or in IT design. Designed with care and consideration, with intelligence and a view to form, function and use. Whether we admire the piece itself or not we can and should pay respect to the creator.

When we don't acknowledge that things are designed in a corporate space, we invalidate the process that it takes to actually create them.

Once we do that, we underappreciate the people that undertook the process to create amazing things in the first place.

It's sometimes easy enough to do. When we don't understand the how, we can't fully appreciate the what.

Sometimes the fact that an item is so big, different, and loud (in any sense of the word), we can't ignore the art behind it. Whether it's a car or a rocket or something else.

Many times, we ignore the art because we can't see it or understand it.

That is unfortunately human nature. However, we are talking here about a corporate environment, so there should be someone who can understand the inspiration and perspiration put into everyday roles that create things that are amazing as well as truly functional.

To be anywhere near that and as a manager or colleague and not identify it and appreciate it is to the complete detriment of the entire company.

This corporate attitude to our creation is what kills the spirit inside of us.

Have I created anything that is truly "great art"? No, sadly not yet. But I have spent many years creating things which are never acknowledged. Sure, I get paid to be there, to create and implement. But when we spend our time creating something that is misunderstood it's a death of 1000 cuts.

Maybe this sounds overly emotional to apply this to a job you do for money. But think about all the colleagues that resigned, disheartened and bitter.

"Nobody appreciates what I do"

"I'm given half the time and half the budget I need"

I've heard it and felt it so many times. And as with many artists it is only after those employees are gone that we fully appreciate them.

Need more proof? How many programmers save their best work for the open-source projects they work on at night and the weekends?

Embracing the inner artist

O pen-source code. A lot of it is done by volunteers, after corporate work is done. By all accounts, peer reviewed open-sourced code is improved and refined into some of the best in the world.

I imagine after a long slog of programming something at work, our open-source programmer gets home, opens up a special code project. This project is not like his corporate code. It's careful and deliberate. It's his baby. It's treated well. Thoroughly and endlessly reviewed and refined.

There's no ding of an incoming email, or reminder popup of the next meeting. His workspace is whisper quiet. Purposefully so. He doesn't even attempt to code until dinner is done and cleaned up, the kids are in bed and the wife is engrossed in her own hobbies. This is his time and it is spent creating his masterpiece.

I knew a surgeon once. He told me that after a day of surgery, back in hallowed grounds of their lounge, all the surgeons gather to relax and regroup. They also like to show off. One after another hangs up an x-ray of a surgery from the day to show off their impeccable skills. A beautify reconstruction here, an amazing repair there. Extremely capable hands performing world leading surgery. The x-rays were the proof. My surgeon friend tells me it gets to him, and his surgery wasn't the best or the neatest. His x-rays weren't a proud testament to his achievements. This helped to prompt him into another career, and he is happier for it.

I wonder if we all got to peel back the layers of our work and hung it up next to others for all the other expects to see, would we feel proud of our accomplishments, or would we make and excuse to leave before it was our turn.

Not every server rack is beautiful and not every line of code is a masterpiece. Not every line of code needs to be. But it would be nice to work in an environment that encourages us to do our very best work every day.

I think that would be an extraordinary place to work. It sounds like a dream land, but I suspect even the smallest of changes can help to make our work better and our satisfaction higher.

As a space nerd, I've watched all the movies and TV shows about the American Space program in the 50s and 60s (and 70s, 80s etc). I find the technology amazing and the challenges they faced seemingly insurmountable. Not living through it I started out knowing the end before the beginning which ruined the surprise ending (they made it to the moon and back, wow!). If I had lived through that period, I imagine I would be quietly hopeful but internally sceptical of the chances of getting to the moon and back.

One thing that stands out to me through this time is the amount of dedication astronauts in particular put into the program. It was their entire world. From sunrise to sunset, to moving to Houston, to training, to endless hours studying. Everything was focused on getting onto a crew and going into space.

Afterwards, the fallout was clear. Of those 60s Gemini and Apollo astronauts, many were burnt out. Not many marriages survived the intense pressure. Those that accomplished amazing feats were left feeling helpless. What do you do next after walking on the moon? How do you pick yourself up for a new challenge when the funding is all dried up?

We hear a lot of talk about work/life balance. It's an extremely tricky thing to get right. On the one hand work pays for things. On the other life spends all that money living.

It's far too easy to chase one before the other.

But I think there is a different pressure that people don't really discuss in looking at the balance.

Lots of people gain a major satisfaction from their work life. Some days, work is actually really fun, and satisfying. You create something new, you overcome a challenge. You enjoy spending time with colleagues. This is not acknowledged enough. We sometimes spend years looking for a great work environment, and when we find it, we get told to go home more often. WTF?!?!

Financial pressures dictate that those of us not independently wealthy essentially need to have a job. There can be enormous pressure to do the long hours and put in large amounts of effort to retain a role and thus overcome financial pressure.

Sometimes going home is not actually fun at all. Sometimes we don't like the people in our home, especially sad when it's our family, or partner or children. Sometimes, there's no one to go home too.

Our whole identity can be tied to our job. There is nothing apart from what we do for a living.

An often-overlooked aspect is people can become institutionalisation through work. As discussed for lots of people change is unimaginably scary. Even a workplace that is not a great one for many reasons, can provide a safe unchanging environment to be comfortable in. The thought of changing jobs can be so excruciatingly difficult to even consider. Even if we love to complain about the bad coffee the poor parking and the way the sun comes through the window at a bad angle through June. There is an enormous amount of comfort in this stability. It's our bad coffee, we know the good parking spot and how to get the best desk for a better view.

For some people, the institutionalisation is useful. Having a static work environment helps deal with changes outside of work. For lots of people it's a great excuse to never try and do anything else.

If you're a manager it's up to you to decide who needs what help. As an IT person responding to their tickets, you might want to overcome the annoyance factor and become friends with these people, because they might just outlast you in the workplace.

In the age of start-ups and the "fail fast" mentality in workplaces, a different workplace pressure can appear. It becomes the pressure of creating something "world-changing" and I suspect 99% of people using this term are not creating anything that will be in any way "world-changing".

I'd probably throw the term "killer-app" in there as well.

Not to be so bold, as others have been in the past, to suggest that everything great has already been invented. Or to say everything is merely a copy or refinement of something else "a fax machine is just a waffle iron with a phone attached". Thanks Grandpa Simpson.

It's just that this excuse is thrown around a lot to inspire people to work very, very, hard.

However, very few things do in fact change the world and are worth spending quite so much time on them. Even things that many people say are indeed life changing do come with a cost as history has shown with Apollo. Was it worth the cost?

At best people are working very hard on the basis they will become very wealthy if the company is the next Facebook or Uber.

At worst, people in a team somewhere are being urged to work really hard "for the good of the company", with their only incentive being getting to keep their job and potentially not being asked to work this hard again.

All of this makes my bullshit meter spike as it's most likely driven by managers desperate for results to drive their own career at the expense of their employees.

The only world changing that's going to happen is your world when you've neglected it at the sake of work.

Here's the problem out in the workplace. People complicate everything. They have ambitions, dreams even aspirations. Bastards! They don't perform 100% 24x7 and have things like families that have the audacity to want them to spend time at home!

For anyone contemplating these larger questions of personal fulfillment in the workplace and work/life balance, or better yet contemplating it on behalf of those who work for you, I'd say, let's take a step back and a deep breath.

What are you trying to accomplish in life? What is your business trying to accomplish? Better yet what do you think you or your business able to accomplish?

Maybe you are going to the moon or mars and really are doing work that is life changing. You are young, few personal commitments and are working in a place that allows you to do some of your very best work.

If you are then great for you. Keep at it.

Most likely you are not. Some tough questions need to be faced. What is the real expectation for you company? Is it really to be the world leader in "x"? Or would it be enough to be moderately successful at "x" to make yourself moderately wealthy?

What's your work expectation? Is it to be in a workplace that values your talents and pays you a comfortable wage?

That's some basic stuff. Nothing world beating.

Let's take it further. Do you as a leader, truly value your employees? Is the success of your company more important than the success of your employees?

I'd suggest that making money is one thing, but building successful people is the real value you can provide as an owner, manager, leader. Bringing in people, helping to building them up to be better than when they started. Providing a place for them to do their very best work. Helping them at the right time to go onto the next step of their career.

That would be the true measure of success for a leader.

Can you imagine working in an environment where people truly believed that was possible, important, and part of the core business values?

Everyone says that people are the greatest asset, but what if you started measuring yourself as a leader based on the personal and workplace growth of your team.

I believe that would be truly "world-changing" for the people that worked for you.

It would require a large amount personal emotional investment on your behalf. And it wouldn't be easy, in fact if your fully invested in it, it will be the single toughest thing you ever do. But even if your only moderately successful at it, it might be the single most satisfying thing you ever do in your career.

Businesses can be frustrating places to be in. Often we are hampered by the people around us, above us etc. But when we have great leadership at any level it can provide an environment where people can be inspired to do truly world-changing work.

Working in a post-COVID World

Waking up and finding yourself in 2021, you look around and see a very different world than 2019. That's where then this book started and since then it's a slight understatement to say that things might have changed slightly since then.

In this light it's easy to understand why I mention hanging out in the break room, which now takes on a completely new meaning.

Far from a bustling epicentre of corporate social interaction, my break room is a fairly empty kitchen in my house. Gone is the fun banter of colleagues enjoying their break, to be replaced with the empty cries of dirty dishes.

There is a new paradigm of working from home. This is not 100% new to most IT people, as we have tended to breach this bold new world of post-office productivity.

However, having our colleagues join us in the work from home world is for many companies an entirely brand new way of working.

In this brave new existence, a lot of the social interactions we had are now gone. Now more than ever is it critical to continue to improve our social connections, not just leave them by the wayside.

It's time to re-evaluate how we are interacting with our colleagues and team and go beyond the simple weekly video call.

So take the core of my message and apply it to whatever situation you find yourself in. Putting on a suit for a Zoom call may entirely overkill, but are you still making an effort in these meetings.

Do you turn up on time and prepared?

Is your office well setup, neat and tidy?

Does it look like you are ready to work or does it look like you're sitting in bed with a laptop on your lap?

Remember, it's not about the fancy suit and tie, it's about making an effort to show you are worth being taken seriously.

In a work from home world, making an effort is still required. What that looks like is going to change. It will constantly change as you change, progress, and grow into new and exciting new roles.

Working from home doesn't mean doing the bare minimum[1]. There's still work to be done. Demonstrating you understand this and can adapt to the challenges it presents, is a clear indicator to those around you that you are a force to be reckoned with.

Not even a global pandemic can stop you.

Be a leader in difficult times. It can be difficult to gain the momentum of an office working by yourself at home. Maybe the routine of getting into work attire, when everyone else is in their pyjamas, helps to get you're into your groove. If it does, then go for it. Wear a suit or a collared shirt and get going. Don't let everyone "slumming it" pull you down.

When teams are pulled apart in a physical sense, it's more important than ever to ensure communication is still happening and clear. It's no different than the other remote teams you've ever had to work with. However, these days the options for staying connected are greater than ever.

It doesn't need to be constant video calls. it can be quick chats via mobile, a VOIP call, a online chat or anything that helps to communicate what you would normally communicate if you were in the office.

This point is critical. If you find yourself at home never speaking to anyone, then your out of the

---

[1] The web logs certainly show a different story for some employees these days

loop. It's possible the loop has in fact disintegrated and is no longer in existence.

This is bad, and the loop needs to be kept intact and functioning for the sake of everyone.

My rule of thumb is, every time you get a tea or coffee from the kitchen at home, consider giving someone a call or reach out in a chat.

If you were in the office and went for a coffee break, you'd most likely ensure you checked in with at least one or two people on the walk to the kitchen and back. Now that you're at home, why is this any different?

You might get some weird reactions to colleagues you call *"just to see how they are going"*. Never give up the opportunity to have those discussions, especially when your colleagues might just need a chat every other day, just to give them someone to talk to. Looking after everyone's mental health is especially important these days. A phone call can be a literal lifesaver.

Wrapping It All Up

Information Technology is evolving into its difficult teenage years as an industry. IT as a career is massively interesting, constantly changing, challenging from all manner of aspects, and never-endingly frustrating. For all of those reasons we will retain an eternal love/hate relationship.

My purpose in writing this book, is to provide some guidance in a range of areas that are entirely non-technical in their nature. Not one Windows vs Linux debate in here at all!

By doing so my aim is to get you thinking about different aspects of IT as a career, and how you operate within your role, company, and career.

Some of you might vehemently disagree with some of my opinions[1], and that's fine and heathy. Plus, if two IT people ever agreed on everything it

---

[1] Wearing a tie will always be a point of contention

would cause a crack in time or something. However, I would ask you to reflect on your own career and consider its health and momentum.

- Do you feel unappreciated in your role?
- Do you feel like your career has stagnated?
- Have you bounced around from job to job?

If any of these ring true for you, then is it time to adjust your mindset a little and try just one or two new things?

It doesn't have to be a complete makeover of your personality, don't hide who you are. Consider that how you interact in the workplace, how you approach your job, and your day-to-day activities may need some tweaking to put you on a better path.

Changing these aspects of ourselves can be very difficult. However, I hope there are one or two things that I've talked about which you can identify with. Things that either are completely new and start you thinking about aspects of your workplace or career that you've never thought about before. Maybe a concept that you've never been able to quite put into words, that you can now clearly vocalise and expand on.

Either way, I hope you learnt something, were challenged by something or had an idea reconfirmed for you.

I don't expect everything in here to be a home run light bulb moment, but I hope there are some nuggets of insight to help you along your journey.

Maybe you thought you wanted to be the next global powerhouse of a CIO, building infrastructure, and coding the next Facebook, Twitter or Uber but on reflection you realise you just like writing code and all that management stuff seems like it's not really your cup of tea.

Good for you!

Understanding these things can be difficult and tricky. The biggest obstacle is being honest with yourself about your own likes, dislikes, goals, abilities and potential.

People work best in the role that works best for them.

Learning what that role actually is for each one of us, can be harder than actually finding the role to start with.

Being a CIO is only one path. And a fairly indistinct one at that. No two CIOs are the same and neither are their roles.

"Finding yourself", by travelling the world in some aimless pursuit of self-discovery is in of itself a completely stupid concept. Founded I imagine in preoccupation of narcissism and a massive preoccupation in your own self-worth. If I ever wrote a book that claimed to be the IT version of Eat, Pay, Love then kill me quickly and publicly shame me.

However, personal growth and understanding through honest self-reflection and interrogation, without the 12 month world perfectly blogging tour, is critical to self-development.

The ability to continually be self-critical, self-evaluating, and not just from a negative sense by any means, is essential to being purposeful in your own career and life. This doesn't have to be a minute by minute, day by day breakdown. But it's helpful and heathy to be reviewing yourself, your life, career, personal happiness etc.

Everyone obviously is different. Some will prefer a more relentless pursuit of improvement. Others will prefer a more happy-go-lucky means to existence. I'm sure there's a happy medium between both.

However, I think it's important to go through the process in some way shape or form regularly before you realise you've spent 20years in a single job at the same desk doing the same thing waiting for an opportunity to do great work.

Everyone else gave up on that company "with so much potential" and moved to another which was using its potential.

20 years at the same company is perfectly fine if you finish your time and have no regrets. But make sure you reflect on your situation to ensure you aren't having them.

There are deep questions here around personal fulfilment, the division and priority of career vs family etc. Most of these questions fall outside of the scope of what I wanted to write in this book as they inevitably relate to issues mostly not related to IT and IT related careers.

The most important thing to flag, is that each one of us should stop and pause regularly and question the position we find ourselves in. Is it where we think we should be? Is it putting us on a path that meets with our plans and/or aspirations? Are we stuck in a rut due to inaction?

I know there are lots of reasons why moving out of a role is difficult. However, don't be stuck in a role for longer than you need to be, simply due to your own inaction.

Moving roles can be difficult. Finding the right role is challenging at the best of times. Knowing you are in the wrong role, or aspiring to a different one is, however, the start of getting to the right place.

IT can be a difficult career for many reasons. We've covered some of them, and I'm sure you've identified with many. The happiest of workplaces can be stressful, so the not-so-happy ones can be downright horrible. At the end of the day people are more important than any job they do.

So, whatever you do, remember to look after yourselves and your colleagues.

I believe nerds, geeks and IT people in general have the potential to do amazing things. History has shown that those that have come before us have already done some monumental things. The wave of IT invention is by no means over, it's only just really getting started. We are already a part of it in our own way, however, big or small.

Because of the advancements made before us, it is easy than ever before to do more and more great things. The barrier to entry has never been lower.

Ultimately, the greatest investment we can make today, and tomorrow is to keep working on ourselves and helping those around us. Our greatest accomplishments may never be the infrastructure or code we build but the people we help to shape.

About the Author

Rob Hogarth is an IT consultant based in Sydney Australia with over 20 years of working in IT companies large and small.

He is the owner of Monpearte IT Solutions (Mon-pea-art) and mstore.com.au

His focus is building amazing infrastructure, secure systems and transforming applications. He also occasionally is known to write some code.

When he's not working he can be found flying planes, building rockets, and racing cars, sometimes he even goes outside.

You can find out more at:

robhogarth.com

monpearte.com.au

mstore.com.au

Printed in Great Britain
by Amazon

33001875R00118